*Uniforms of the Ala*  *...ion*

*1835-1836*

*Also by the Author*
Uniforms of the Republic of Texas and the Men that Wore Them 1836-1846

# *Uniforms of the Alamo*
## *and the Texas Revolution*
### and the Men who Wore Them
### 1835-1836

Bruce Marshall

**Schiffer Military History**
Atglen, PA

*On the front cover:*
**TRAVIS** by Bruce Marshall. In the background is the Alamo chapel and Travis' letter of appeal of February 24, 1836, described by more than one historian as the most heroic document in American history (the artist has shown both sides of this single sheet, which was written on both sides).

*Dedicated to Joseph Hefter*
*Meticulous researcher and artist, whose knowledge of the uniforms of Texas, Mexico, Spain in the New World and the Maximilian era surpassed all others; an historian generous to a fault in sharing his knowledge with others.*

*Acknowledgments*
Especially helpful in encouragement, guidance and assistance in locating otherwise unfindable records and documents were: Brigadier General Jay A. Matthews, Jr., publisher of Presidial Press and *Military History of Texas and the Southwest*, and Editor Emeritus of its successor, *Military History of the West*; Christopher La Plante, State Archivist and his able staff at the Texas State Archives; John M. Thiel, MD, Chief of Naval Operations, the Texas Navy; Kent Biffle, Texana columnist of the *Dallas Morning News*; the late Major General Thomas S. Bishop, former Adjutant General of the Texas National Guard; Dr. L. Tuffly Ellis, past Director of the Texas State Historical Association; Jane L. Tanner, Associate Editor of *Military History of the West*; Billy Bob Crim, President of the Texas Navy Association; former State Representative Bill Blythe; former Speaker of the Texas House of Representatives Bill Clayton; Colonel John R. Elting, Texana expert of the Company of Military Historians; fellow artist-historian Jack Jackson; the late artist-historian Tom Jones; Mike Koury, publisher of the Old Army Press; and the late artist-historian Joseph Hefter. And especial gratitude to my loyal staff – all family – son Randy Marshall for preparing the maps, his wife Ann and my other son Cody Eanes Marshall for computerizing the text.

Book design by Robert Biondi.

Copyright © 2003 by Bruce Marshall.
Library of Congress Catalog Number: 2002112999.

Printed in China.
ISBN: 0-7643-1778-4

We are always looking for people to write books on new and related subjects. If you have an idea for a book, please contact us at the address below.

Published by Schiffer Publishing Ltd.
4880 Lower Valley Road
Atglen, PA 19310
Phone: (610) 593-1777
FAX: (610) 593-2002
E-mail: Schifferbk@aol.com.
Visit our web site at: www.schifferbooks.com
Please write for a free catalog.
This book may be purchased from the publisher.
Please include $3.95 postage.
Try your bookstore first.

In Europe, Schiffer books are distributed by:
Bushwood Books
6 Marksbury Ave.
Kew Gardens
Surrey TW9 4JF
England
Phone: 44 (0)208 392-8585
FAX: 44 (0)208 392-9876
E-mail: Bushwd@aol.com.
Free postage in the UK. Europe: air mail at cost.
Try your bookstore first.

# *Foreword*

The Military Forces of the State of Texas are very fortunate in having Bruce Marshall to chronicle their history and their uniforms. Their uniforms reflect their glory as well as their adversities. Having been an independent nation and a state in two different nations, the diversity of their military forces, Navy as well as Army, is unequaled. All of this is shown in his paintings. His research and his talent are impeccable and truly inspire others, who so disposed, to excel in their work. Those of us who have served in this unique military force are sincerely grateful to Bruce Marshall.

John C.L. Scribner
Brigadier General (TX) (Retired)
Command Historian
Texas Military Forces

# *Introduction*

The notion has persisted far too long that the army of patriots that won Texas independence from Mexico in 1835-1836 was totally without uniforms, clad indifferently for the most part in rustic frontier garb, homespun shirts, jackets and trousers of buckskin and colorful coonskin caps, looking like the cast of a John Wayne movie. This was true for many, but by no means all. Surprisingly, there were uniformed Texas units in all of the major battles of the Texas Revolution from the first to the last: the siege of Bexar, the Alamo, Goliad (Coleto), and the final astounding victory at San Jacinto.

This is the long overdue history of the uniforms of the Texas Revolution and the men who wore them.

It will also reveal certain hitherto suppressed material from some who served, including the vast majority of the Texas officers, challenging the generally accepted historical version portraying the Texas commander, General Sam Houston, as a master strategist who, alone, deserved full credit for saving Texas.

Only recently have serious scholars looked behind the veil created by Houston sycophants and examined these sources seriously. No less than the number one authority on Texana until his mysterious murder (or was it suicide?) in 1989, John H. Jenkins, in editing *Amasa Turner's Account of the Texas Revolution* acknowledged, "Most of the anti-Houston material in the past fifty years has – and this is quite true – been deliberately and designedly prevented from coming into print."[1] Still another crack, albeit only a hint, in the Paul Bunyon-like mystique surrounding Sam Houston is almost hidden in a footnote in *Texian Iliad* by Stephen L. Hardin. "The time has come for scholars to set aside the hagiography penned by political hacks and hero worshipers in order to gain a fresh perspective on the 'Sword of San Jacinto' and his role in the campaign."[2]

Herein is the full, balanced story, all the more dramatic shorn of the glossy, sugar-coating presented by school texts and tourist brochures. An army, assembled to fight and eager to close with the enemy, discovered, to the dismay of almost all, that their chosen leader had the opposite intention – *flight*. Their commander-in-chief had his own personal demons to contend with in addition to the advancing Mexicans and his difficult to control army – alcohol and possibly opium addiction. Before the final showdown between Sam Houston and his officers and soldiers, half of the volunteers had deserted from lack of confidence in his leadership. The remainder were in a mutinous mood, determined to force "Old Sam" to lead them into battle – or fight without him by the time they arrived at their rendezvous with history at San Jacinto.

At last, for eighteen explosive minutes late in the afternoon of April 21, 1836, the Texas Army, both uniformed and non-uniformed companies, took their destiny in their own hands, ignoring most of the commands of their reluctant and irresolute leader and, following their own instincts, totally routed an enemy twice their size. Today, at the base of the San Jacinto Monument is this inscription:

> Measured by its results, San Jacinto was one of the decisive battles of the world. The freedom of Texas from Mexico won here led to annexation and to the Mexican War, resulting in the acquisition by the United States of Texas, New Mexico, Arizona, Nevada, California, Utah, and parts of Colorado, Wyoming, Kansas, and Oklahoma. Almost one-third of the present area of the American nation, nearly a million square miles, changed sovereignty.[3]

This is the story, more fascinating than fiction, of those desperate and determined heroes, in their, for the most part, home-made uniforms or tattered rags of frontier clothing, and who fought both the army of Mexico and their own commander and – incredibly – prevailed over both; though the latter appropriated their laurels in the history books.

# Chapter One

# *Background*

**The Arrival of the Anglos: A Clash of Cultures**

The uniforms of the Texas Revolution, and later the Republic of Texas, have their origins in the conflict which arose between the Anglo-American settlers, who began to colonize in Texas from the 1820s into the 1830s, and the several governments of Mexico which ruled Texas during those years.

Though Anglos had participated in expeditions into Texas and revolutionary activity under Spanish and Mexican rule earlier, and various Anglo squatters had moved in before, the truly significant Anglo penetration began with the settlers led by Stephen F. Austin. Approval to settle Anglo colonists had been obtained June 10, 1821 by Moses Austin, Stephen's father, from the Spanish authorities in the waning months of the colonial regime. Moses Austin died before being able to begin his settlement of Anglo families. But his son took over management of his project and brought the first of the three hundred families contracted for to Texas. In the meantime, Spanish authority had been supplanted in Mexico by revolution. It was not until 1824 that confirmation of Austin's *empresario* grant was bestowed by Mexican authorities. Nevertheless, the process of organized Anglo immigration was underway and unstoppable.

Aware that the province of Texas was slipping away due to the inability of the colonial regime to protect its settlers from the native Indians, the Spanish authorities clutched at the hope that settlement of Anglos would be a solution. Especially as the Anglos, in their own land, had proven themselves quite capable of mastering the Indians. In Texas they soon got the upper hand over the Indians and, as one historian observed, during the fifteen years before their revolution had accomplished more than the Spanish or Mexicans had done in one hundred and fifty years.[1] This presented a new problem. Could the Spanish, later Mexican governments, keep the Anglos from supplanting them as well as the Indians? This concern began to curdle the attitude of succeeding Mexican governments toward the newcomers. Suspicion fostered excessive fear. Second thoughts of the wisdom on continued Anglo settlement sharpened and gradually, while going through the motions of still welcoming them with one hand, Mexican officialdom began to take steps to choke off the immigration with the other hand. Their alarm grew as the Anglo population outnumbered Mexicans in Texas by more than ten-to-one by 1828, according to one Mexican official's alarmed report.[2]

Anglo was an inclusive description for the new settlers, mostly from the United States, of predominately English, Scottish, and Irish stock, with significant minorities of German, French (particularly Huguenot), and later Czech. Predominant were those from the Southern states. These latter brought with them Black slaves.

Serious differences of culture, race, religion, morality, and political orientation began to manifest themselves from the beginning. All of the colonization grants required the *empresarios* to bring only those of the Roman Catholic faith. Virtually none were, except for those recruited by two Irishmen, John McMullin and James McGloin, who settled Irish families at San Patricio. Neither Austin nor any of the other *empresarios* made any attempt to comply with this requirement. Austin, always eager to have good relations with the Mexicans, continually admonished his followers to respect the Catholic faith, at least outwardly. Privately, he referred to the faith of the Mexicans as "bigoted and superstitious to the extreme," with a "fanaticism" that "reigns with a power that equally astonishes and grieves a man of good sense."[3] As for the Mexicans themselves, the majority were "rabble,"[4] according to Austin, and "indolence seems to be the order of the day."[5] His attitude was charitable compared to most of the Anglo settlers. One of them, William B. Devees, observed "The Mexicans are never long at peace with each other; ignorant and degraded as many of them are, they are not capable of ruling nor yet of being ruled."[6] Creed Taylor, later a captain in the Texas Army observed, "I looked upon the Mexican as being of an inferior race, domineering, lazy, vindictive and treacherous ... there was no more harm in killing a greaser than slaying a Commanche."[7] Still another colonist, Noah Smithwick, was even more blunt, "I looked upon the Mexicans as scarce more than apes."[8]

Interestingly enough, this attitude towards the Mexicans of Texas was shared by a cultured Mexican official sent to Texas in 1828 with a commission to report on the state of affairs there, General José Manuel Rafael Simeón de Mier y Terán. It was to be a fateful mission darkening the fate of Anglo settlement in Texas. Mier y Terán, a member of Congress, had with him a staff and escort including two lieutenant colonels to survey the military situation, Constantino Tarnava and José Batres (the latter to die in the Battle of San Jacinto), Jean-Luis Berlandier as botanist, Rafael Chovell serving as zoologist and physician, and Sub-Lieutenant José Mariá Sánchez, his aide-de-camp, a virulent anti-American, who also served as draftsman and artist.

The commission entered Texas February 1, 1828 at Laredo. After a stay there, it proceeded to San Antonio, then capital of Texas, then eastward to the American border, pausing to visit Austin's colony at San Felipe de Austin. As Mier y Terán and his observers made their way eastward from San Antonio, where most of the Mexican population lived, they became increasingly disturbed by what they saw: *Anglo colonists taking over.* Mier y Terán's impression of the local Mexican inhabitants and officials was almost identical to that of the Anglo settlers. They were, he reluctantly recorded, "the lowest class – the very poor and very ignorant" and their officials "venal." The foreigners, on the other hand, were "more aggressive and better informed," he reported, and more "shrewd."[9] Both groups, unburdened themselves on Mier y Terán. "The colonists murmur against the political disorganization of the frontier, and the Mexicans complain of the superiority and better education of the colonists," he wrote to Guadalupe Victoria, the president of Mexico, in a personal letter under date of June 30, 1828 while still in Texas, "It would cause you the same chagrin that it has caused me to see the opinion that is held of our nation by these foreign colonists ... I tell myself that it could not be otherwise than that from such a state of affairs should arise an antagonism between the Mexicans and the foreigners."[10]

Mier y Terán foresaw immediately the inevitability that, unless checked, the foreigners, as he called the Anglos, were going to take Texas away from their host. Or, as Noah Smithwick put it in his usual plainspoken bluntness, "It is not in the nature of things for the superior race to long remain under the domination of the inferior."[11]

For the next several years Mier y Terán agitated every high Mexican official to the danger, as he saw it, of the Anglo menace, urging counter-measures. In 1829, for instance, he shrilled, "If the colonization contracts in Texas by North Americans are not suspended, and if the conditions of the establishments are not watched, it is necessary to say that the province is already definitely delivered to the foreigners."[12]

His loyal aide Sánchez, the only member of the commission who was with him throughout their entire Texas tour, echoed Mier y Terán's dire warnings and fear of the Anglos. While feigning friendship towards Austin in their relations with the *empresario* in person or by correspondence, both Mier y Terán and Sánchez saw him and his colony, which was the best administered, as therefore the greatest threat. "In my judgment," Sánchez predicted darkly, "the spark that will start the conflagration that will deprive us of Texas will start from this colony."[13] Mier y Terán and his staff managed to color and cloud the attitude of the national government towards the Anglo Texans and, more than any other factor, poison the relationship. While Texans of the time and later historians cast Antonio Lopéz de Santa Anna as the great nemesis of the Anglo-Texans, in truth it was Mier y Terán who was by far their greatest and most effective enemy, the man most influential in setting the stage for confrontation and conflict.

His efforts to undermine the Anglo colonists reached full fruition with the passage of the Decree of April 6, 1830. *This repressive law, designed to choke off Anglo immigration to Texas and substitute a counter-colonization by Mexicans and others, was the turning point in relations between the Mexicans and Anglos.* Mier y Terán deserves full credit for it. Virtually all of its provisions were based on his recommendations. His intimate friend, Lucas Alamán, Minister of Interior and Foreign Relations, congratulated him, gushing, "Nothing has been done but to make extracts from and coordinate different paragraphs of your communications on the subject."[14]

On January 1, 1830, another old friend, Anastasio Bustamante, had become president, and virtually the entire cabinet was now Mier y Terán cronies. Mier y Terán was elevated to the dual positions of Federal Commissioner of Colonization and Military Commander of the Eastern Interior Provinces, which included Texas. *He now had full authority to enforce the decree.*

Among its most onerous conditions were: a virtual halt of immigration from the United States; favoritism for colonization by Mexicans and Europeans, mainly Swiss and Germans; an oppressive military occupation, which would include convict-soldiers, to suppress any Anglo resistance. Especially dismaying to the Anglos was that the convict-soldiers and their families would be settled in Texas and encouraged to remain as colonists when their term of service was up, plus civilian settlers would be recruited partly from Mexican prisons. Texas, the American colonists learned, was to become the dumping ground for the dregs of Mexico.

When news of the decree reached Texas, Austin tried to put the best face on it. Still at this point the loyal sycophant of Mexican sovereignty, he published in the *Texas Gazette* an editorial professing to see great benefit from the decree, glossing over its dark side. The garrison of occupation would give added protection from the Indians, he glowed, ending with the preposterous assertion, "This effort of the government to protect and foster the infant settlement of this remote member of the union, affords an additional proof of the paternal care of the General Government towards the inhabitants of Texas. If ever there was a people who have reason to be satisfied with their government, it is WE, the people of Texas."[15]

If Austin was really sincere in such sappy rapture, his colonists were not deceived. From that point forward, they knew they were on a collision course with the Mexicans.

All that followed, the long litany of grievances claimed by the Anglo-Texans until full conflict erupted in 1835, emanated from the Decree of April 6, 1830, and the government's effort to enforce it. The Anglos, now calling themselves *Texians*, and who now were about twenty thousand of the twenty-five thousand population,[16] had now to act in self-defense or lose all they had worked to establish since entering Texas.

# Chapter Two

# *The Texas Revolution and its Uniforms*

M istrust, born of the Decree of April 1830, spread throughout the Texian settlements. It was fanned by harsh enforcement of the decree by administrators sent to Texas: Colonel John (who called himself Juan) Davis Bradburn (despite his Kentucky origin, more Mexican than any Mexican), George Fisher, described as either of German or Serbian origin, Colonels José de las Piedras and Domingo de Ugartechea, and General Martín Perfecto de Cos, the brother-in-law of Mexican President Antonio López de Santa Anna, and others.

A war party formed among the Texians. Prominent in it were William Barret Travis, Patrick C. Jack, Andrew Briscoe and R.M. Williamson, the latter called "three-legged Willie" because of a deformed leg that necessitated his wearing an additional artificial one.

Austin headed the peace party, striving until nearly the last for Texas to remain a part of Mexico.

Small clashes at Anahuac, Victoria, Velasco, and elsewhere built up to the conflagration warned of by Sánchez, but the spark that truly ignited it flared at Gonzales, not at Austin's colony as he had predicted.

The dispute was of relatively minor significance, a demand from the Mexican authorities at San Antonio for a return of a small cannon given to *empresario* Green De Witt years before for defense of his colony against the Indians. Scarcely more than two feet long, it was hardly worth fighting over, but by then anything could have set off the inevitable revolution. A small group of Texians defied the dragoons sent to retrieve the cannon. Their women had prepared a flag with a saucy message to taunt the Mexicans: COME AND TAKE IT. In the resulting skirmishing the Mexican soldiery was sent flying back to San Antonio without the cannon.

The skirmish over the Gonzales "Come and Take It" cannon on October 2, 1835, became the "Lexington of Texas." Militia assembled at Gonzales, then marched on San Antonio for a reckoning with General Martín Perfecto de Cos, commander of the Mexican troops in Texas.

Now even the pacifical and normally conciliatory Stephen F. Austin bowed to the inevitable and even accepted command of the newly formed army. To David G. Burnet he had recently written privately, "No more doubts – no submission. I hope to see Texas forever free from the Mexican domination of any kind."[1]

Until now only a single uniform had been authorized for Texas, that of the civic militias of Coahuila and Texas while they were combined into one political entity. Created in 1834, the regulations designated:

Article 82. The Uniform of the militia shall be coat, pantaloons and cap of deep blue, collar, cuffs and lacing yellow, with yellow buttons for the infantry, and white for the cavalry; no militiaman shall be compelled to wear uniform even in actual service but in this he must not be without a cockade, equipment and the necessary arms.

Article 83. While the funds of the militia are not sufficient to defray the expense of uniform, its use shall be discretional and those who have the means and wish to wear it will perform a laudable and patriotic act by doing so.[2]

From this it is obvious that militiamen, other than perhaps officers, were not realistically expected to be uniformed because of financial lack, both governmental and personal. Furthermore, there is no evidence that it was worn in Texas, at least not by the Anglo settlers in revolt against Mexico. Until now, the Texians had depended entirely upon their own non-uniformed militia and, of course, the regular Mexican troops stationed in Texas for their defense against Indians. The Texians citizens militia was informal and without supreme command or superstructure. An old settler described them as "minutemen, ready to enter service at a moment when called upon."[3] Organized originally for defense against Indians, the citizens militias now became the nucleus of the new Texas Army.

The only professional military force in the Anglo colonies to this point was a small mounted unit, called *rangers*, personally hired and paid from his own pocket by Stephen F. Austin to protect his own colony headquartered at San Felipe de Austin. These ten men were the original Texas Rangers.[4]

The popular impression of the clothing of the Texians during the Texas Revolution has always been that of the frontiersman, civilian garments, often deerskin. This was reinforced by a number of contemporary descriptions. "Rags were our uniforms. Nine out of ten of them were in rags," was the recollection of Valentine Bennett, quartermaster of the Texas Army, when asked about uniforms.[5] Nevertheless, uniforms appeared and were worn in all of the major engagements, as we shall see. By the time of the final battle, San Jacinto, a sizeable portion of the Texas Army was uniformed.

There were none yet, however, as the newly formed Texas Army took the field, about five to six hundred strong, as they marched behind the diminutive "Come and Take It" cannon.[6] According to Noah Smithwick, it bore little resemblance to the army of his childhood dreams:

Buckskin breaches were the nearest approach to uniform, and there was a wide diversity even there, some being new and soft and yellow, while others, from long familiarity with rain and grease and dirt, had become hard and black and shiny. Some, from having passed through the process of wetting and drying on the wearer while he sat on the ground or a chunk before the campfire, with his knees elevated at an angle of eight-five degrees, had assumed an advanced position at the knee, followed by a corresponding shortening of the lower front length, exposing shins as guiltless of socks as a Kansas Senator's. Boots being an unknown quantity; some wore shoes and some moccasins. Here a broad-brimmed sombrero overshadowed the military cap at is side; there a tall "beegum" rode familiarly beside a coonskin cap, with the tail hanging down behind.[7]

## The First Uniforms

Joining the patriots marching on Bexar were the Lynchburg Volunteers, thirty strong, all outfitted in matching suits paid for by a wealthy planter, William Scott. Exactly what the suits looked like is unknown. The Bruce Marshall illustration of the Lynchburg Volunteers in *The Ten Battle Flags of the Texas Revolution* is only speculation.

The first truly uniformed unit appeared in time for the siege of San Antonio de Bexar, the New Orleans Greys.

★   ★   ★

*Plate 1 (page 53)*
### THE NEW ORLEANS GREYS

Two companies of volunteers were raised in New Orleans to aid the Texians, each designating itself as the New Orleans Greys. They were described as men of many nations.

Their uniform was similar to the fatigue uniform of the United States Army, but grey instead of the American azure blue. It had black trim instead of the white of the

U.S. uniform. Their garrison cap was black *sealskin* – not, as wrongly illustrated in other works, the U.S. model 1826 forage cap, which was *ribbed cloth*. Confirmation of sealskin as the correct cap is found in a letter to his mother from Sergeant Ebenezer S. Heath of the Greys. "The color of our uniforms was a grey jacket and pants with a *sealskin* cap."[8]

Both companies were uniformed, but it has been a matter of debate whether their uniforms were custom-tailored for them or some obsolete militia uniforms found in depots in New Orleans. Suggesting the latter is this translation by Lothar Frommhold of the University of Texas at Austin from a book in German by Herman Ehrenberg of the first company of the Greys. "As soon as possible all of us took possession of Grey clothing … these clothes we found ready-made in some of the numerous warehouses and the name of our squadron stems from these grey clothes."[9] Reinforcing this is a letter from the captain of the second company, William Gordon Cooke to his brother, located by Edward Miller, a San Antonio history teacher whose special interest is the Greys, which mentions that *only four days elapsed* from the formation of the second company to their departure.[10]

The first company, led by Captain T.H. Breece, marched to Texas afoot. On crossing the border they received their flag from a pretty Texas lass among their greeters, according to Ehrenberg. This was the only Texas banner to survive the battle of the Alamo. It is shown behind the Grey in Plate 1.[11]

At Nacogdoches, the first company was served a feast and mounted on donated horses. They rode the balance of the way to Bexar (which then was the popular designation for San Antonio).

The second company arrived by sea, also to a tumultuous welcome. Its leader, Cooke, was to play a long and dramatic role throughout the military history of Texas. He also made an advantageous marriage to Angela Maria de Jesus Blasa Navarro, niece of José Antonio Navarro,* a prominent aristocrat of San Antonio, who sided with the Anglo colonists and held many important posts. Cooke and his uncle-in-law were also two of the three commis-

sioners appointed by Republic of Texas President Mirabeau B. Lamar to accompany the Santa Fe Expedition. Along with the others of the Santa Fe Pioneers (as expedition members were called) they were captured and jailed in Mexico.

Sixty-five Greys left New Orleans. Four joined along the way. By the time the two companies had made their separate ways to San Antonio, a Major R.C. Norris had assumed overall command. At San Antonio their name was quickly changed to the *San Antonio* Greys. History, however, remembers them best as the New Orleans Greys.

★   ★   ★

## The Siege of Bexar

Austin, on arrival, wanted to immediately storm the city. But inexplicably the mood of the officers and men had changed from cocky confidence to caution. While styling themselves the "Army of the People" they were at this point little more than an undisciplined mob. Their only artillery was a cannon taken in a skirmish near the mission Concepcion, the "Come and Take It" mini-cannon having been abandoned on the march after its carriage broke down.

## The Debut of Sam Houston

While they were encamped near San Antonio in late October the volunteers were addressed by several leaders. First was Stephen F. Austin. Though without any real military training or experience other than fighting Indians, he had been named general. After Austin came a relative newcomer, Sam Houston, recently elected a delegate from the Nacogdoches area to the forthcoming consultation in November. Houston clearly wanted Austin's job, and meant to get it by whatever means necessary. Houston hammered at three points. "It was easy to discover that his chief wish was, that the troops in the field, should be immediately disbanded," observed Colonel, then Captain, Robert M. Coleman, one of the volunteers. "One of the first acts of the consultation," Houston attempted to persuade them, "should be the appointments of a major general and the provision for a regular army for Texas," and to make a treaty with the Indians. According to

---

*Navarro is credited by virtually all histories as a prominent Mexican leader in Texas. He was, but his parentage was actually Corsican.

Coleman, "He used every art to discourage the army; he even attempted to scare the soldiers to their homes by insinuating that the northern Indians in Texas were about to commence hostilities."[12] Later at the consultation, Houston was to present himself as the only man in the army with the credentials of *major general* and capable of negotiating the treaty with the Indians, as he had for much of his life lived with the Cherokees.

Following this astonishing harangue by Houston, William H. Jack gave a rebuttal, reassuring the volunteers of the necessity of first capturing San Antonio, and rebuking Houston's scare tactics. Jack carried the day.

Mortified by this setback, Houston (probably a manic-depressive by today's standards) went into a depression and, lacking what many came increasingly to suspect were his usual stimulants of "whiskey and opium," according to Coleman, attempted to blow his brains out with a pistol. He was dissuaded with difficulty by James Bowie and Francis W. Johnson. "Such," observed Coleman, "was the conduct of Sam Houston on his first appearance in the army of Texas."[13]

On his way to the consultation at San Felipe de Austin, then the capital of the Anglo settlements, Sam Houston made every exertion to sabotage Austin's volunteer army. Without authority, he ordered cannon and reinforcements headed for San Antonio to turn back. At Gonzales, according to Coleman, Houston "renewed his intimacy with his old associates, Whiskey and opium, in whose society, while at that place he indulged without restraint."[14]

Whatever the stimulus, by the time Houston had reached San Felipe his confidence had returned and he immediately lobbied for the post of major general and the creation of a regular army and the treaty with the Indians. All, he argued convincingly, should be trusted to his hands. He was persuasive. Houston was a handsome giant, a "man's man," hale, hearty, and charming. Sober or drunk, he was awesome to most. Few at the consultation had witnessed his bizarre behavior at the encampment of the Army of the People. And heavy drinking was to some on the frontier a sign of manhood, not a vice, if a man met the other criteria of frontier acceptance. Terán, in his observations, noted that the Anglo Texans worked hard, then often drank themselves into oblivion when their

work was finished.[15] As for the more serious allegation of opium addiction, Houston partisans say this was a misconception caused by his frequent sniffing from a vial of hartshorn on which he depended as a stimulant. Whatever the case, Houston cut a bigger than life figure among the mostly unsophisticated Texians. He had been a protégé of Andrew Jackson, and was highly skilled in the rough and tumble of Tennessee politics. And he knew how to ingratiate himself and fit in with the camaraderie of the grog shop habitués.

There were indignant detractors, to be sure. In an angry letter to the president of the consultation at San Felipe, George Huff and Spencer H. Jack denounced Houston and his "hangers on" as "traitors," and in fact, the country's "worst and most dangerous enemies." Zeroing in on Houston, they charged, "His conduct here has evidenced the most discontented and envious of spirit mixed with the most unmeasured vanity." After reciting instances of his efforts to discourage the volunteers and to turn back reinforcements, cannon and supplies from reaching the army in the field, they characterized Houston as "a vain, ambitious, envious, disappointed, discontented man, who desires the defeat of our army – that he may be appointed to the command of the next."[16]

Houston, however, played his ace. He had been a major general of Tennessee militia, the only one of the Texians to have held such a high military rank, or anything close to it. He boasted, "I will discipline my troops and make them as invincible as were the veterans of Napoleon."[17] He made a virtue of his dissolute life among the Indians and that he had been the adopted son of the Cherokee chief Bowles by presenting himself as the emissary best qualified to negotiate peace treaties with the Indians. He won.

## Houston Takes Command

Houston was made Major General and Commander-in-Chief of a national army, to consist of 1,120 men, plus 150 Rangers. No uniform was as yet designated. In accord with Houston's design, the Army of the People besieging San Antonio was curiously left unprovided for.[18]

Also created was a *state – not national –* government. This and a declaration that they were fighting for "the republican principles of 1824" were setbacks for those favoring independence. A governor was chosen, Henry Smith, strangely enough an independence advocate, and a general council was created.[19]

Until now Stephen F. Austin, the foremost *empresario* who has guided the Anglo-Celtic colonists through all of their formative years from the 1820s had been clearly their leader. But at the consultation Sam Houston had cunningly outmaneuvered him and was now the undisputed leader of the Texians. Austin, his humiliation complete, departed to seek funds in the United States.

Edward Burleson now became commander at Bexar. A man with a repuation as a rough and tumble fighter, he now proved strangely irresolute. He did nothing. While the siege dragged on into winter, the uniformed Greys, both companies now united, grew restless. They wanted to fight or leave.[20]

The situation deteriorated to the point where the officers, with the exception of Francis W. Johnson, Adjutant and Inspector General of the Staff, wanted to abandon the siege and go into winter quarters at Gonzales. In all likelihood this would have destroyed the army and the revolution. Fortunately, the day they were to leave a Mexican deserter, a Lieutenant Vuavis, brought word that morale was low in the city and it could be taken by a resolute assault. A force was quickly raised by Johnson and Benjamin Milam, an *empresario* recently escaped from a Mexican prison who had joined the army on the march to Bexar. On December 5, they attacked. Johnson led one unit, which contained both companies of the uniformed New Orleans Greys. Milam headed a second unit, with Major Morris of the Greys as second in command.

The uniformed and better disciplined Greys were the shock troops, performing feats of valor mentioned in Johnson's report of the battle. They had only one casualty, a private Breeden, seriously wounded while spiking a cannon. The Mexicans surrendered after four days of fighting. Burleson, who had remained in camp furnishing logistical support and reinforcements, signed the surrender document, and then resigned. Johnson, now the hero of the hour, became head of the volunteers. As one of his first acts, he petitioned the council for an appointment in the regular army for Captain Cooke of the Greys.

Together with Dr. James Grant, a former Scottish highlander regimental officer, Johnson next proposed to carry the war to the enemy by an attack on Matamoros, a port on the south side of the Rio Grande. Some of the Greys, led by Major Morris, went with him. Others of the Greys, with their flag, remained at San Antonio.

During all this time the man who had been named as Commander-in-Chief of the regular Texas Army by the General Council, Sam Houston, was noticeably absent. He had done nothing to assist the campaign against Bexar, in fact had worked against it. He now bestirred himself and from his headquarters issued a proclamation calling for volunteers. In it he referred to those at San Antonio as *the Army of the People*. Those under his command he called *the Regular Army*. Part of the army, according to his appeal, was to be an *auxiliary volunteer corps*, also under him as Commander-in-Chief. By this he sought to gain authority over all Texas forces, including Johnson and James W. Fannin, at Goliad, who at this point were pretty much acting on their own.[21]

On December 16, the council created a cavalry of 384 men under Travis, and a Ranger force of 168 under R.M. Williamson.[22]

Thus was the Texas military organized at last, at least on paper. But rivalry continued as to who would become the ultimate leader. In some ways the rivalry was more deadly than the enemy.

## Santa Anna Declares War of Extermination

In the meantime, Santa Anna declared a war of extermination on the Texians. To his commanders he instructed:

> The foreigners who are making war on the Mexican nation in violation of every rule of law, are entitled to no consideration whatsoever, and in consequence no quarter is to be given them, of which order you will give notice to your troops.[23]

In late December, on instructions from Santa Anna, his Secretary of War had a circular distributed in the United States intended to intimidate Americans from assisting the Texians. It warned that any foreigners found in Texas with arms in their hands or who sent supplies to the Texians would be treated as pirates and shot. In the words of historian Louis J. Wortham, "the issue was thus sharply drawn. The outcome could only be one of two things: either the Anglo-Americans would be massacred or driven across the Sabine, or an independent Texas, entirely separate from Mexico, would emerge from the war. There was no longer any middle ground."[24]

## Clothing Arrives

On January 28, a load of supplies was sent from New Orleans via several vessels by Texas purchasing agent Edward Hall. In addition to military equipment, it included clothing: "400 russet brogans; 1,200 mens kip (untanned hide) brogans; 36_ doz. canteens; 1 case Irish knit half hose; 200 cartridge boxes and belts; 30_ doz. jackets; 30_ doz. pantaloons; 47_ doz. socks; 62 doz. shirts; 1 doz. kersey pantaloons; 2 doz. heavy twilled shirts; 1 doz. check twilled shirts; 1 doz. gingham twilled shirts; 2 doz. white cotton shirts; 1 doz. satinet (a thin inferior satin, especially one containing cotton) vests; _ doz. satinet vests (perhaps a different kind of satinet vest?); 24 suits satinet; 1_ doz. red flannel shirts; 3 flushing pea coats; 4 doz. woolen half hose; 1 doz. brogans."[25] Hall and other Texas agents were buying any clothing they could get their hands on, whether military or not.

That some of these supplies were received and issued to the troops is evidenced by a receipt given shortly after by Jones M. Townsend to Governor Smith at San Felipe for: 23 pair brogans; 2 jersey round jackets; 3 pair satinet pants. A notation on the receipt shows the clothing was distributed among thirty soldiers, and their names are listed.[26]

About this time is another receipt, though undated, signed by Captain T.M. Allen who brought "emigrants" (volunteers) with him on the schooner *Equity*, acknowledging receipt of: 60 cavalry swords; 14 doz. banyan jackets; 2 doz. pantaloons; 100 knapsacks; 3 cases 72 muskets and bayonets.[27]

Following the victory at Bexar, and for want of something to occupy the restless patriots and especially the volunteers, the idea of carrying the fight to the enemy by an attack on Matamoros gained favor. Though he was later to deplore it as a hair-brained scheme, the idea had

occurred to Houston as well as Johnson. On December 17, he had sent an order to James Bowie to gather a force and attack the port.[28] Bowie, however, had hurried from Goliad to join the volunteers converging on San Antonio and did not learn of Houston's message until January. Captain Philip Dimmit of Goliad had written to governor Smith also urging an attack on Matamoros. It also had appealed to Austin.

The various rivals for military leadership converged on Goliad in January. Each was determined to gain control and become the savior of Texas: Houston, Fannin, and Johnson and Grant, who now styled their followers the *Federal Volunteer Army of Texas*.[29] Fannin won control of the troops at Goliad. Reaching an accommodation with Fannin, Johnson and Grant moved on to the vicinity of San Patricio on their way to Matamoros. Houston, the big loser at this point, skulked back to San Felipe to lick his wounds and await developments. Some of the Greys under Major Morris accompanied Johnson and Grant. Others stayed with Fannin.

## Another Uniformed Company

Until now the Greys had been the only uniformed company. At Goliad another uniformed unit appeared: the Alabama Red Rovers.

★   ★   ★

*Plates 2 and 3 (page 54 and 55)*

## ALABAMA RED ROVERS

Most of the Red Rovers came from around Courtland, Alabama. They were described as the flower of Southern youth. Their captain, older than most of his recruits, was Dr. Jack Shackleford, a veteran of the War of 1812. Such was the enthusiasm across the South for the Texas cause that, despite the neutrality of the United States, the weapons and accoutrements for the Red Rovers were issued from the state arsenal, the United States Cadet musket, Model 1830, with bayonets.

All sixty-one, some say seventy-one, of the Red Rovers were uniformed, but accounts differ as to how. Some remembered their uniforms as being hunting frocks or vests while others contend the uniforms were copied from the fatigues uniform of the American Army. In each case they were red, though descriptions vary from bright red to a reddish-brown or brown. Probably the variation in color was from dyes that were not color fast and which faded to various shades under the brilliant Texas sun.

Both descriptions are more or less correct, as the Red Rovers actually had *two* uniforms, according to the reminisces of Colonel James E. Saunders, whose mother and other ladies sewed the uniforms.

The service uniform was the hunting frock, which had a caped top, sometimes two, covering the shoulders. The frock was elaborately trimmed with fringe, as were the trousers. This costume was patterned after those made popular during the American Revolution by irregular units. Sometimes they were fashioned from deerskin, but usually they were of dyed cloth. Those of the Red Rovers were of "lindsey woolsy" cloth, according to Saunders. Many Texians on the Mier Expediton of 1842 wore similar hunting outfits.

The second uniform, apparently for dress parade, consisted of a red cap and jacket made of velvet, a blue sash, and white trousers. This one was on the U.S. Pattern.[30]

The Red Rovers left the vicinity of Courtland in December of 1835, arriving at Dimmit's Landing in Texas aboard the steamboat *Yellow Stone*. They were accepted in the service of Texas on February 3, 1836. At Goliad, Fannin assigned them to his Lafayette Battalion.

Their flag, shown behind the figures in Plates 2 and 3, was small and squarish, red without ornamentation.

★   ★   ★

Fannin now had over four hundred men under his command at Goliad. Almost all were volunteers from the United States. Only about thirty-five were Texas regulars. In addition to the uniformed New Orleans Greys and Alabama Red Rovers there were several small companies: the Mobile Greys (also known as the Alabama Greys), the Mustangs from Kentucky, the Huntsville Volunteers, Amon B. King's Kentucky Volunteers, some artillerymen, a few "Polanders" and a battalion from Georgia. Whether any of these men were uniformed (except for some of the New Orleans Greys who transferred to the Mobile Greys) cannot be ascertained. The companies were formed into the Lafayette Battalion and it was combined with the Georgia Battalion to make a regiment. The Georgians were equipped with long arms from their state arsenal, like the Red Rovers.

Johnson and Grant now split their force into two more or less equal groups of fifty men each.

At San Patricio on February 27, Johnson and his party were taken completely by surprise by Mexicans under Gen. José Urrea. Most were killed. Only a half dozen or so escaped, including Johnson.

Grant, with Major Morris of the New Orleans Greys, and presumably some of the Greys, was also taken by surprise on March 2, while rounding up horses near Aqua Dulce. Only three escaped. Among these was the Alcalde of Victoria, Plácido Benavides, who hurried back to Goliad to warn Fannin the enemy was now at hand.

How many of the Greys died with Grant and Morris is uncertain. Some were still with Fannin at Goliad while others remained in San Antonio with the Grey's flag.

During March, Felix Huston, who was active in the United States throughout the revolution raising men, munitions, and money, reported from Natchez that he was planning to start for Texas with five hundred *emigrants*. "I am making preparations for arms, ammunition, uniforms, etc., etc. at an expense of $40,000. I intend to arm and uniform the men well."[31] The euphemism of calling volunteers emigrants was to circumvent the neutrality provision of the treaty between the United States and Mexico.

Tragically, but not surprisingly, there seemed to have been mishandling of the desperately needed supplies sent from the United states. Two letters – only a day apart – give us a clue. The first is from John S. Brooke at Goliad, dated March 2, to his mother: "We are all nearly naked – and there are but few of us who have a pair of shoes."[32] At Velasco, the Assistant Inspector General, George W. Poe, had a problem of too much. On March 3 he wrote: "There is a large supply of arms, ammunition and clothing here," but complained there was no one to take charge of it or protect it.[33]

By March, Captain Cooke of the New Orleans Greys seemed to have worn out or discarded his uniform. An entry of March 5 in the diary of colonel William Fairfax Gray, a Virginia gentleman traveling Texas scouting for favorable land deals, observed prisoners being "brought under the care of Captain William G. Cooke … Poor Cooke was badly off for a wardrobe, and Waller and myself were happy to supply him with such of ours as we could spare, which he received with thanks and without any false shame."[34]

In San Antonio the remaining soldiers, under Colonel James C. Neill, were reinforced by Bowie and a handful of volunteers. Travis also arrived with about thirty regulars. David (Davy) Crockett, the legendary frontiersman, arrived also with his Tennessee Company of Mounted Volunteers. But this raised the defense force to only about 150 men, totally inadequate to man the large quadrangle that comprised the Alamo.* The Alamo had cast a spell over all who commanded it. None could bring themselves to obey Houston's order to blow it up and retreat. There was, in their eyes, good reason. "The salvation of Texas depends upon keeping Bexar out of the hands of the enemy," Bowie wrote to Governor Smith. "Colonel Neill and myself have come to the same conclusion, that we will rather die in these ditches than give it up to the enemy."[35] Travis, too, saw Bexar as "the key to Texas."[36]

There was much to be said for this from a military standpoint, despite Houston's aversion to defending forts. At the Alamo was the largest collection of artillery (twenty-one guns) between Mexico City and New Orleans. It would have been utter folly to abandon this, the Texians' greatest military asset, without resistance. Plus, if the enemy could be stopped at Bexar the Anglo settlements eastward would be spared the ravages of war.

Though the Bexar defenders knew the Mexicans were coming, they nevertheless were surprised to discover on February 23 that the enemy was only a few miles away. At sighting of the Mexican vanguard the Texians hastily pulled back into the Alamo compound and prepared for siege.**

## The Alamo

Santa Anna's army, including reinforcements following, consisted of 4,473 infantry, 1,024 cavalry, 182 artillerymen, 185 sappers, 60 presidials afoot and 95 mounted: more than 6,000 men. The Alamo defenders numbered 150.[37]

Santa Anna demanded surrender. Travis answered with a cannon shot. Now began the most heroic defense in the history of North America and perhaps the world.

Were any of the defenders of the Alamo uniformed other than the New Orleans Greys?

Of Travis' regulars, "only he alone wore a regular uniform,"[38] according to Lon Tinkle, author of *Thirteen Days to Glory*. Other historians are less certain.

Travis may have been uniformed, according to Texana expert Colonel John R. Elting, and some of his regulars may have been semi-uniformed.[39]

It is documented that Travis ordered a uniform for himself and gave instruction for uniforms to be procured for his men. In a letter to Captain W.C. Hill at Velasco, under date of January 21, 1836, he advised:

> I have this day sent you orders about contracting with McKinney (& Williams of Quintana) for our uniforms and equipment. I wish you to attend to it immediately. I spoke to him about my uniform, which I have written to him to purchase.[40]

This was more than a month before the Mexican army encircled the Alamo. Did Travis' uniform reach him, or the uniforms for his men, reach the Alamo before then? We can only conjecture.

---

*What tourists are now shown as the Alamo, and what appears on all the picture post cards, it should be mentioned, is only the original chapel. The chapel was only a part of a mostly walled enclosure comprising several buildings. The principal building was actually the Long Barracks, not the chapel, which is the only other original building remaining. The Long Barracks, now a museum as is the chapel, is however greatly altered in form, reduced from its original two stories to one. The other buildings now on the grounds of the Alamo are not original.

**According to one romantic but unlikely bit of folklore, Santa Anna, in disguise, attended a fandango in the town attended by some of the Texians the evening before his army was sighted.

★　★　★

*Plate 4 (page 56)*
## COLONEL WILLIAM BARRET TRAVIS

No solid clues exist as to the color or cut of Travis' uniform. But there is the possibility he may have known he was to be appointed as the colonel to command the Legion of Cavalry, and that the uniforms of the army, including the cavalry, were to be gray, actions under the discussion by the General Council which had assembled March 1 at the Washington on the Brazos.[41] Messengers were continually slipping in and out of the Alamo during the siege, carrying out appeals, bringing back news, as late as three days before the final assault. So the best, but by no means certain, guess is that Travis' uniform was, as shown here, gray with yellow buttons, as formalized by the Council.

Reinforcing this assumption is advice on Travis' uniform from a contemporary, Alamo expert Rueben Marmaduke Potter, to the historical artist Henry A. McArdle. "Travis, if dressed as a lieutenant colonel of this nominal cavalry corps, would have worn a short swallow-tail, pantaloons and forage cap, with facings, stripes and a band of black." But he added, "I doubt if he had obtained such a uniform."[42]

The several paintings of Travis in existence, including the one in the Travis County Courthouse, show him in a blue swallow-tail (as on the cover) with a lone star on the left breast. Probably all of these were done posthumously. The only known contemporary likeness of Travis is a pencil sketch done before the revolution attributed to his friend Wylie Martin.

Another remote possibility exists. In an inventory sent to the General Council of clothing for the army is shown: 366 jackets and 366 pairs of pantaloons (color unspecified), 570 pairs of socks, 62 shirts, 200 cartridge boxes and belts, 440 muskets, 100 carbines, 50 pairs of pistols, 75 sabres. These were at Brazoria or Velasco.[43] Considering that Captain Hill was at Velasco, and that Travis had ordered him to forward uniforms *immediately*, there is the chance that Hall might have forwarded some of these items on to the Alamo.

Behind Travis is the Alamo chapel as it was during the siege. The top already was damaged, perhaps part of the destruction done by Texian gunners during the siege of Bexar before Cos surrendered. The profile atop the Alamo now was put on by the United States Army Corps of Engineers in 1848.

★　★　★

Now began a siege which was to last for thirteen days. Though surrounded, Travis managed to send out messages appealing for aid. The most dramatic, still preserved in the Texas Sate Archives, has been described by more than one historian as "the most heroic document in American history."[44] It is worth repeating in full:

*Commandancy of the Alamo –*
*Bejar, Feby. 24, 1836 –*

To the people of Texas
        & all Americans in the world –

Fellow Citizens & Compatriots – I am besieged, by a thousand or more of the Mexicans under Santa Anna – I have sustained a continuous bombardment & cannonade for 24 hours & have not lost a man – the enemy has demanded a surrender at discretion, otherwise, the garrison are to be put to the sword, if the fort is taken – I have answered the demand with a cannon shot, & our flag still waves proudly from the walls – <u>I shall never surrender or retreat</u>. Then I call on you in the name of Liberty, of patriotism, & everything dear to the American character, to come to our aid, with all dispatch – the enemy is receiving reinforcements daily and will no doubt increase to three or four thousand in four or five days. If this call is neglected, I am determined to sustain myself as long as possible & die like a soldier who never forgets what is due to his own honor & that of his country –

VICTORY OR DEATH
William Barret Travis
Lt. Col. comdt

P.S. The Lord is on our side – when the enemy appeared in sight we had not three bushels of corn – we have since found in deserted houses 80 or 90 bushels & got into the walls 20 or 30 head of beaves –

Travis[45]

On February 28, James Fannin, the commander at Goliad, in response to the appeal from Travis set out half-heartedly with three hundred men and four cannon to reinforce the Alamo. But only a few miles out he thought better of it and turned back.

From Houston, nothing was heard.

On March 1, in the dead of night arrived the only reinforcements that ever came, thirty-two courageous patriots from Gonzales under Captain Albert Martin. One had a blind wife and eight children. The number of Alamo defenders was now 182.

Puzzled by the delay of Fannin, Travis sent another messenger to him, James Butler Bonham. At Goliad Bonham was informed by Fannin that no help would come from Goliad, where a Mexican column under General José Urrea was expected. Bonham, in one of the most courageous acts of the revolution, told Fannin that Travis and the Alamo defenders deserved to know that no aid would be coming from Goliad, (which had the largest concentration of Texian soldiers, and thus was their only real hope), and left to rejoin the doomed defenders.

After midnight on March 3, Bonham, under a hail of Mexican bullets, rode through the gate of the Alamo and delivered the melancholy message: *no help was coming*.

Travis then assembled the garrison and made his now famous *line in the sand* speech. He informed them frankly that no more help could be expected: he was determined to remain himself and, with whomever chose to remain with him, to die with honor. Any who wished to escape might still be able to do so and were free to go. He then drew a line in the dirt, asking those who would remain to cross over it and stand beside him. All crossed over – even Bowie, who was ill and dying and asked some to lift his cot over the line – all except one: a French Jew known as Moses Rose (real name Louis Rose).[46] Rose made his escape during darkness and lived to tell the story of *the line in the sand*.

To keep up the spirits of the doomed defenders David Crockett played his violin and a Scotsman, John McGregor, played his bagpipe.

In the early morning of March 6, 1836, Santa Anna assembled his troops for the assault. For many nights he had created false alarms so as to keep the defenders edgy and exhausted. Now the attack was to be carried out silently, so as to effect maximum surprise. The three Texians posted outside the walls to watch for such a silent approach had been disposed of without noise. It might well have succeeded had not some of the Mexican soldiers in their excitement began shouting slogans: "Long live the Republic! Long live Santa Anna! Death to the Texans!"[47] Alerted by the tumult, the Texians were at their posts and ready as the Mexicans surged forward from all sides.

Withering fire from the Alamo artillery and the careful fire from Texian long rifles turned back the first two assaults. But Texians casualties were heavy also. Atop the walls they made highly visible targets.

Travis guessed correctly that the main thrust would be at the north wall, where earlier Mexican artillery had made a breach. Protecting the breach was the de Teran battery. As courageous in deed as he had been in word, Travis had assigned himself the most dangerous post of all – *the de Teran battery*. At the first alarm Travis and his nineteen-year-old Black servant Joe had hurried to the de Teran battery. As Travis leaned over the wall to fire both barrels of his shotgun into the ascending ladder loads of Mexicans, he was struck in the forehead by a bullet, wounding him fatally. He fell back into a sitting position. According to Joe's account, a Mexican general, Mora,* as he came over the wall saw the dying Travis and slashed at him with his sword. Travis, with his last measure of strength, parried Mora's thrust with his own sword and ran the Mexican officer through. They died together at the de Teran battery.[48]

In his famous appeal of February 24, Travis had promised to "die like a soldier who never forgets what is due to his own honor and that of his country." In the admiring words of Mexican military historian General Miguel A.

---

*Probably Colonel Esteban Mora rather than General Ventura Mora. Esteban Mora was assigned to the attack on the north wall (where Travis died); whereas Ventura Mora was patrolling the perimeter with the cavalry.

Sánchez Lamego, "Travis fulfilled his promise. He did not surrender or give up. He resisted to the end and died a valiant warrior on the esplanade of the de Teran battery."[49] All of the Alamo defenders died with him. "Not one of them would surrender," Santa Anna later wrote the artist Henry Arthur McArdle.[50]

All of the historical artists who have painted the subject, except Joseph Hefter and myself, have shown the battle in the dawn's early light. In actuality it was fought in total darkness. By *dawn's early light* Santa Anna was writing his victory report.[51]

Travis was wearing a "jean coat," during the final assault, according to the Mexican sergeant who stripped his corpse and stole it.[52] But most American-style military clothing of the period was made of jean material, so this gives us little clue as to whether it was a civilian or military coat.

**The Alamo Flags**

In his appeal of the twenty-fourth Travis wrote that "our flag still waves proudly from the walls." There has been considerable speculation as to what flag Travis referred to. The flag of the New Orleans Greys was certainly there, but there may have been others. David Crockett is said to have brought one. Travis mentioned having one made for five dollars. This was a Mexican tricolor with the numerals 1824 substituted for the traditional eagle and serpent, according to Sánchez Lamego, who gives a Mexican version of the battle in his *Siege and Taking of the Alamo*. This 1824 flag is the one most favored by historians and artists. It would represent that the defenders were fighting for the "republican principles of 1824" as resolved by the provisional state government in November. Sánchez Lamego asserts there were *at least* two flags at the Alamo, the 1824 flag and the blue banner of the New Orleans Greys. Further confusing the issue is a sketch of the Alamo attributed to Lieutenant Colonel José Juan Sánchez Navarro, who participated in the siege, showing a Mexican tricolor with two stars in the center, one above the other. This, some reason, stood for the combined entity of Coahuila and Texas, a view supported by Vito Alessio Robles in his *Coahuila y Texas*, according to Sánchez Lamego.[53]

There was hand to hand fighting around a flag flying over the Long Barracks, called El Cuartel (the Quarters) by the Mexicans. Several Mexican soldiers died attempting to tear it down. Sánchez Lamego seems unclear whether this was Travis' 1824 flag or the Greys flag. However, according to Luis Castillo Ledon, in 1935 director of the National Museum of Archeology in Mexico City, where the flag was kept for a time, "The flag was a light blue and placed at the highest point of the Alamo when the Mexicans attacked the fort. Three men of the Jimenez Battalion were shot down while attempting to tear the flag of the New Orleans Greys down from the topmost point of the Alamo and set the Mexican flag in its place."[54]

However many flags were or weren't at the Alamo, Santa Anna sent back only one with his victory report: the blue banner of the New Orleans Greys. But the curious wording of his report suggests there might have been others. "The bearer takes with him one of the flags of the enemy's battalions, captured today. The inspection of it will show plainly the true intention of the treacherous colonists, and of their abettors, who came from ports of the United States of the North."[55] It has been conjectured that he sent only the Greys flag because the message on it would prove connivance between the colonists and sympathizers in the United States. It would have been an embarrassment to include the 1824 flag, if it was taken also, because that might arouse sympathy for the colonists among Mexican liberals who also supported the constitution of 1824.

The flag of the New Orleans Greys was passed about between several museums in Mexico city for some years. Brigadier General Jay A. Matthews, Jr., a military historian specializing in Texana and for many years publisher of *Military History of Texas and the Southwest*, recalls seeing it at one time in the Chapultepec Palace. Over the years there have been several efforts to have it returned to Texas. Several Mexican flags captured at San Jacinto or elsewhere have been offered in exchange. The Mexicans have always stubbornly spurned such offers. In the meantime, the flag has suffered serious deterioration and when last seen was almost unrecognizable. The latest effort to retrieve it was in 1994 by Texas state senator Carlos Truan, hoping that the North American Free Trade Agreement (NAFTA) reached that year might soften Mexican hearts. Perhaps annoyed by this persistence to the point of exasperation and hoping to close the matter forever, the answer from the Mexican authorities was that the flag had been lost in the shuffle between museums and now cannot be located. It is a hardly plausible explanation, one few Texans will be satisfied with.[56]

## Uniform Fragments in Urn?

A final macabre footnote on the uniforms of the Alamo defenders came in 1936, the year of the Texas Centennial, when a coffin or urn was exhumed from the San Fernando cathedral in San Antonio. According to Colonel John Elting, it contained some charred bones and uniform fragments, supposedly of the Alamo garrison.[57] It can only be speculated as to whether these were uniforms of the New Orleans Greys, Travis' regulars (some of whom might have enlisted still in their old U.S. Army uniforms left over from the recent Florida Indian campaign, in the opinion of General Jay Matthews), or Travis' own uniform, or a combination of these. This receptacle may have been the one containing such remains Juan N. Seguin claimed to have placed in the cathedral shortly after the bodies were burned by order of Santa Anna.[58]

The heroes of the Alamo perished without knowing that the General Convention, four days before the fortress fell, had declared Texas independent. It also created a constitution, elected as interim president David G. Burnet, as vice president Lorenzo de Zavala, and again confirmed Sam Houston as Commander-in-Chief, with rank of major general, to have power over all Texas forces: regulars, volunteers, and militia.

The provisional government established by the convention, which lasted from March 1 to the 17, made provisions for an army, navy, marines, militia, and a Legion of Cavalry. It also provided for munitions of war and provisions for the military.

## Uniforms Provided

Uniforms were to be bought: 2,000 grey suits, with proper number for sergeants, corporals, etc.; 2,000 colored cotton shirts (while the color is not specified, later Quartermaster General inventories show these as brown); 2,200

pair of yarn socks; 2,000 pair of brogans, sizes 6-12; 200 sergeants swords with belts. Cavalry winter uniforms were to be: suits of cadet grey cloth coats with yellow bullet buttons, pantaloons and fur caps; For summer: two suits of grey cottonade roundabouts (a waste-length jacket) and pantaloons. Also, black cloth socks and cowhide boots. Half of the Legion of Cavalry was to be equipped with twin-barrel shotguns, the other half with American Yagers, all flintlock. Each cavalryman was to have a broadsword, a brace of "substantial" horsemens pistols with brass-mounted holsters (horsemens pistols differed from regular ones by having a swivel joint holding the ramrod to the barrel so the ramrod wouldn't be lost when reloading while mounted) and a belt and cartridge box. Also to be purchased were: 100 Spanish Oppelousas saddle trees with red blankets; 100 bridles; 100 surcingles; 100 cabristras; 100 pairs of stirrups and spurs. Among other essentials were 3,000 pounds of Kentucky chewing tobacco, 120 gallons of French brandy and 120 gallons of Port wine.[59]

William Pettus was authorized to purchase for the Volunteer Army of the People of Texas then in the field: 666 pair of warm pantaloons; 666 cotton shirts; 666 pair of socks; 333 vests; and 333 round jackets.[60]

These supplies were to be obtained by Texas agents in the United States. But though money was appropriated for them it is unclear if they arrived, at least in any appreciable quantity. At any rate, the choice of gray as the color of the field uniform set the pattern for virtually all subsequent field uniforms of the Texas Army.

Some of the terminology used in the descriptions of uniforms should be explained. Cadet grey has a slight blue tint (like the uniforms of most military academies). Pantaloons for today's readers has the connotation of loose, baggy trousers such as worn by zouaves or the bloomers of the suffragettes; but in the nineteenth century pantaloons was merely a synonym for pants or trousers. Booties were not short boots, but a high-topped shoe with laces at the top. In military use, the *Jefferson Bootie* was especially popular throughout most of the nineteenth century. Just what a *Spanish Oppelousas saddle* looked like has modern historians stumped.

## Houston Drags His Feet

The fate of the Alamo was as yet unknown elsewhere in Texas when on March 4 Sam Houston received noticed of his renewed commission. With the greatest reluctance he prepared to go to Gonzales to take command of the 400 or so men congregating there to go to the relief of the Alamo. He took his time, reaching Gonzales on March 11, a six day journey which could have been made in one or two days. He claimed there was no hurry because the reports from Travis from the Alamo were lies, and those from Fannin of approaching Mexicans were also lies, meant to improve their popularity over his.[61] According to Creed Taylor, a spunky fighter and later a principal in the infamous Sutton-Taylor feud, "We could have reached him (Travis) in two days, by March 5 at the most."[62]

At Gonzales Houston found pandemonium. Two Mexicans had brought the word of the fall of the Alamo. This was confirmed shortly by the arrival of Mrs. Susanna Dickinson and her baby girl, Angelina, escorted by Travis' black servant, Joe.* Mrs. Dickinson was the widow of Captain Almeron Dickinson, the artillery officer at the Alamo. She had been with him in the Alamo, and she and Joe were spared by Santa Anna so they could tell of the massacre and, hopefully, panic the Texians into flight. This psychological ploy was highly successful.

Among the first to panic was Houston. "He became much agitated and showed every symptom of fear, he would sometimes rave like a madman, at other times seemed much dejected," according to Robert Coleman.[63] By all accounts he hastily dumped the army's only two cannon into the Colorado River without spiking them (from which they were fished out soon after by the Mexicans). He ordered the town burned as well as outlying farmhouses. All equipment that could not be transported was burned, including tents and camp baggage. The haste was so great pickets posted three miles west of town were not called in, and many families were left behind also – including the blind Alamo widow with eight children. Thus began in the words of Creed Taylor, "the most disgraceful retreat ever recorded in any history."[64]

## Another Uniformed Unit Arrives

At Gonzales a third uniformed unit joined the ranks of the Texians, the Newport Rifles, volunteers from Kentucky under Sidney Sherman.

★   ★   ★

*Plate 5 (page 57)*

## COLONEL SIDNEY SHERMAN
### Kentucky Volunteers
### Newport Rifles

Sidney Sherman was a manufacturer of bagging at Newport, Kentucky when the Texas Revolution began. He was also captain of the local militia company, the Newport Rifles. Deeply interested in the Texas cause, Sherman sold his business and personally financed a military company to go to the aid of the Texian rebels. It is believed the Newport Rifles volunteered *en masse*, and made up most, if not all, of the volunteers Sherman raised for Texas. They wore "traditional uniforms," according to the *Southwestern Historical Quarterly*.[65] Elsewhere they are described as being "well armed, handsomely uniformed and fully equipped."[66] Whether they wore the uniforms of the Kentucky militia or new uniforms furnished by Sherman is unclear. Also unclear is whether theirs were a more modest version of his own uniform (probably the latter). Uniforms of the militia of the period might have been patterned after those of the regular army, but not necessarily. Many militia companies of the day were quite imaginative in design and, more often than not, not in conformity with the national forces. Sherman had his portrait painted in 1835, while still in Kentucky, wearing his uniform.** The coat and vest and other of his memorabilia are preserved in the San Jacinto Monument. This incomplete uniform and that of Major General of the Reserve Thomas Jefferson chambers, also only a coat plus some accoutrements (also placed recently in the San Jacinto Monument), are all that is extant of the many uniforms of the Texas Revolution and the Republic of Texas.

---

*A second Black, accompanied Mrs. Dickinson, Ben. But Ben was not in the Alamo. He was a servant at Santa Anna's headquarters and was sent with the Alamo widow as an escort by the dictator.

---

*The uniform in the portrait, however, does not exactly match the one in the San Jacinto Monument. He may have had more than one uniform.

There were approximately fifty two men in the company, but only thirty of them uniformed when they embarked for Texas on December 29, 1835, according to the *Cincinnati Daily Whig* of that date. The *Whig* added the hope that "uniforms for the remainder of them can be made on their passage down the river provided the liberality of our citizens furnished them with the materials."[67] The thirty uniformed men may have been the original Newport Rifles and the rest additional volunteers. According to another newspaper, "they numbered about fifty in uniform, and each man supplied with a good rifle." The company "made a handsome appearance," according to the newspaper, "with their beautiful banner waving over them, having on it the motto 'liberty or death.'"[68]

This flag was made by the ladies of Newport and presented to the company at a farewell ball. The flag bearer was James A. Sylvester, whose sweetheart gave him one of her gloves as a talisman. He tied the glove atop the flag staff. Flag and glove were carried by Sylvester at the battle of San Jacinto. It was the only flag carried by the Texas Army during that final battle which won the war. What became of the glove is unknown. The flag was given by a grateful Texas to the wife of Sidney Sherman. Later, Sherman descendants donated it back to Texas after statehood. It is now displayed behind the speaker in the Texas House of Representatives. This flag is shown behind Sidney Sherman in Plate 5 and also behind the United States volunteer in Plate 9 as the flag they fought under.

James Sylvester is also remembered as the leader of the patrol that captured the dictator Santa Anna the day after the battle of San Jacinto.

The Kentucky volunteers were described as "the most reckless, drunken, and lawless men in the Texas army," by Mexican Colonel Pedro Delgado, later their prisoner after San Jacinto.[69] But at San Jacinto they proved to be among the bravest.

★ ★ ★

## Goliad
Meanwhile at Goliad, Fannin now received an order from Houston to abandon Fort Defiance and retreat. Like those

in the Alamo, his men had put a lot of effort into improving the long neglected presidio, which Fannin had renamed Fort Defiance, mounting and positioning its fourteen guns to best advantage.[70] Nevertheless, bowing at last to Houston's supreme authority, he began foot-dragging preparations to comply.

On March 18, a Mexican army under General José Urrea appeared before Goliad. The next morning, Fannin began a sluggish retreat towards Victoria. In the van marched the uniformed Red Rovers behind their rust red flag. The uniformed New Orleans Greys were the rear guard.

Such cannon as he took along and other supplies were pulled by oxen, slowing them to a snail pace. This bothered some, but not Fannin. His contempt for the Mexicans and their fighting ability from his experiences at the siege of Bexar was so great he didn't believe they would dare follow. But on the prairie the Mexicans cut off his column and surrounded it. He had made the fatal mistake of stopping for a rest in the open – *just a mile and a half short of protective timber and water*. After a day's fighting in an engagement called the Battle of Coleto by the Texians and Encinal del Perdido by the Mexicans, he surrendered.

That the Greys and Red Rovers were still in their uniforms at this time is confirmed by the account of one of the surviving Greys, Herman Ehrenberg:

Curiosity had drawn many Mexicans to our camp, where they eagerly examined the heaps of gleaming rifles surrendered by our men. Our tawny foes looked timidly at the somber soldiers in grey uniforms who had proven such dangerous adversaries, for most of these Mexicans had not forgotten their strenuous experiences during the siege of San Antonio, and the vivid recollection of the fierce struggle with the volunteers kept alive fears which the sight of a disarmed and defenseless adversary should have removed. Yet if the glances of our visitors reflected the shadow of past alarms, they also betrayed their hatred for an enemy who had done them so much harm.[71]

Ehrenberg remembered the Red Rovers as now being in their "brown hunting vests and trousers."[72]

After being deluded into believing they would be repatriated to the United States, most of the prisoners were marched out and treacherously executed on Palm Sunday, March 27. The number slaughtered was 409, according to Lieutenant Colonel J.N. de la Portilla, who carried out Santa Anna's direct order to do so.[73] Thirty-four were spared. These included Dr. Shackleford, captain of the Red Rovers, and certain other medical personnel needed to tend to the Mexican wounded, or for other reasons such as not being armed when captured. About twenty-six or so escaped. Among those uniformed escapees were six Greys and five Red Rovers.

R.L. Rickson, a grandson of one of the Red Rovers executed, Abishai Rickson, reported the flags captured with Fannin's command "were all carried to Mexico" and the Red Rover flag ended up in a museum in Mexico City. If so, no historian has been able to verify it.[74]

Thus were wiped out with Fannin's regiment the last of the New Orleans Greys and the Alabama Red Rovers. Now only the Newport Rifles remained of the three uniformed companies, though certain individuals had obtained uniforms for themselves as we shall see, and at least one more uniformed group was yet to appear.

## The Armies Face Each Other

Houston had stopped at a point on the east bank of the Colorado opposite Beason's Ferry. He had all the boats brought over to his side of the river including the steamboat *Yellow Stone*. Reinforcements added along the way now brought his army up to between 1,300 to 1,500 men. Camped opposite him on the west bank, but with no way to cross, was General Joaquín Ramírez y Sesma with some 600 to 800 Mexican soldiers. Now, thought many, was the time to turn and fight. If the Texians crossed over and attacked, and things went badly, they could retreat via the boats. The only advantage Ramírez y Sesma had was two cannon, perhaps the two Houston had unwisely jettisoned at Gonzales. For six days they sat facing each other. The Mexican couldn't act, because of high water and no boats; Houston hinted at action, but took none.

The army wanted to fight. But Houston consulted no one and didn't call a council of his officers. Instead, upon receiving the disheartening news of the massacre of Fannin's force, he ordered another retreat. Suspicion grew among officers and men that his plan, if he had one, was to retreat all the way to the Sabine River, hoping to lure the Mexicans into American territory where they would then be dealt with by the United States Army. Along the way every town and farm would be burned so as to leave no sustenance for the advancing Mexican armies. This scorched earth policy would leave all of Anglo Texas utterly destroyed economically. Morale plummeted. Many sought furloughs in order to return to their homes to protect their families. Others simply deserted. Nearly half to two-thirds of Houston's army evaporated at this point.[75] By now many had begun to distrust Houston's abilities, his integrity, and even his valor. In Coleman's opinion, "His chief aim was his personal safety."[76]

They might have been even more disquieted had they known that his title of Major General from the States was questionable. In his former political career in Tennessee he had been elected to the office of Governor and earlier to that of Adjutant General of state militia. The militia position carried with it the rank of Major General. In Texas, Houston had played that card at every opportunity. Texians, most of whom had Southern origins, had the Southerner's traditional awe of titles. They took his at full face value. But in fact, *it was mainly political*. In the regular United States Army he had served only briefly during the Creek War in 1814 under Andrew Jackson, rising only to the rank of Second Lieutenant before being discharged for wounds. Thus his actual regular army rank had been a quite modest one and his actual military training and real military experience very limited and of short duration.[77]

## The Runaway Scrape

Houston now retreated to San Felipe, which was reached on March 28. Since the evacuation of Gonzales, virtually all of the Anglo-Celtic population were now in panicky flight with what belongings they could carry by hand, horse, or wagon. This exodus became known as the "runaway scrape." Property and livestock were abandoned and personal belongings jettisoned en route to increase mobility if wagons or teams became disabled. Worse, villainous scoundrels took advantage of the refugees, stampeding them with exaggerated alarms, and then looting their possessions when abandoned.

Those in flight were not limited to the women, children, and elderly. Virtually the only reinforcements now were American volunteers, gallantly motivated by desperate appeals from Texas agents in the United States. The arriving volunteers from the states had the dismaying experience of passing hundreds of armed Texians fleeing in the opposite direction.

Adding to the growing suspicion that Houston had no true intention of making a stand, were his own actions in trying to turn back volunteers en route. Dr. Nicholas Descomps Labadie, a Canadian doctor who had settled in Texas and now accompanied the army, claimed to have heard Houston send orders that reinforcements that had reached Robbin's Ferry on the Trinity in far east Texas were to halt.[78] Coleman added to this, saying that a written order was sent by Houston via a Major Digges that all arriving volunteers should halt at the ferry to await Houston's retreating army, whose arrival there would be in a few days. This caused the temporary halt there of a large number of mounted volunteers under former Mississippi Governor John A. Quitman, according to Coleman.[79] These reinforcements didn't arrive until after San Jacinto.

The army remained only a day there. Houston ordered the retreat to continue on to Groce's plantation, Bernardo, in the Brazos bottomlands. This raised particularly bitter outcries from his soldiers and the refugees. San Felipe was the capital of Anglo Texas. It should be defended at all costs, many argued. In fact, two company commanders, Mosley Baker and Wiley Martin, mutinied. Making a virtue of necessity, Houston detailed them to defend two crossings of the Brazos. Then he pulled out. San Felipe was burned.

## Santa Anna's Fatal Mistake

Santa Anna in the meantime had divided his force. He led one unit of about 750 cavalry and infantry with one cannon hoping to overtake the Texas government, then fleeing towards Harrisburg (near present day Houston).

Others were to locate and engage the Texas army by separate routes. At this point none of the Mexicans were quite sure exactly where Houston and his army were, but they were convinced, as were many of the Texas soldiers themselves, that the Texas commander had no intention of making a stand, but instead would retreat until past the Sabine. At the plantation of Jared Groce, the wealthiest man in Texas, Houston gave his army the rudiments of drill and some discipline, which they needed but didn't care for. He now had only about 500 or so highly dissatisfied men. During the two weeks the army spent there in the Brazos bottomland, eating Groce's corn and cattle, Secretary of War Thomas Jefferson Rusk arrived with a message from the interim President, David G. Burnet:

> Sir: the enemy are laughing you to scorn. You must fight them. You must retreat no further. The country expects you to fight. The salvation of the country depends on you doing so.[80]

It expressed the feelings of most Texians, including Houston's army. But there was a certain grim humor to it, as President Burnet was fleeing faster than anyone. He was now at Harrisburg near the coast. If Houston didn't stand and fight, Rusk was authorized to take command of the army himself. Houston reluctantly called in Coleman and instructed him to circulate among the soldiers and say that, pressured by Rusk, he would, at the fork in the road ahead take the south road – leading to Harrisburg – rather than the other which led to the border with the United States. But few expected him to keep this promise.[81] Many hoped that Rusk would take over then and there, but instead he stayed with the army, joining it.

There was open talk that, if Rusk would not take charge, the Commander-in-Chief should be replaced nonetheless. Favorites were Sidney Sherman, now a lieutenant colonel, and another aggressive hawk, John S. Wharton, the Adjutant General. Houston was well over six feet tall,* a handsome imposing man's man, and a char-

---

*Most histories describe Houston as 6'4"; one sycophant even claiming 6'6". However, Houston's biographer Marquis James, in *The Raven*, says Houston's U.S. Army record shows him as 6'2".

ismatic speaker, with an ego equally as large as himself. He dressed in civilian clothes with a hat whose brim was rolled to resemble that of a revolutionary war tricorn with a cavalier's plume. Both Sherman and Wharton, while not as impressive physically or in eloquence, were each nattily outfitted in smart looking uniforms, which gave them a certain appeal in addition to their hawkish boldness.

★   ★   ★

*Plate 6 (page 58)*

## COLONEL JOHN S. WHARTON
### Adjutant General
### Texas Army

Colonel John A. Wharton was the Adjutant General of the Texas Army. Both he and his brother, William, were early settlers and identified with the war party. John, frequently a critic of Sam Houston, was impatient to fight and may have been the one to bring on the engagement at San Jacinto by agitating the army to near revolt if battle wasn't commenced that day. It is believed by some that his ultimatum to Houston on the twenty-first of April forced the Commander-in-Chief's decision to fight. Wharton was described as tall, wiry, and about thirty years old. He wore a "well tailored blue uniform with brass buttons and a pair of respectable boots, and a most unmilitary Mexican sombrero." Instead of a military canteen he used a Spanish gourd.[82] This was a gourd with an hour-glass shape. Usually a rawhide thong went around the middle, laced to another at the top, and was attached to a strap carried over the shoulder or tied to the saddle. Spanish gourds are mentioned throughout narratives about early Texas. Such canteens were a favorite of the Texas Rangers in particular. They are still used in parts of Mexico.

The cut of Wharton's double-breasted uniform with its golden epaulets in the illustration is taken from a similar one in an oil painting of John M. Allen. They, and perhaps others, had their uniforms tailor-made at their own expense, or possibly obtained surplus U.S. Army issue and may have had them altered to Texian uniforms, mainly by switching insignia and buttons.

Allen, according to records in the Rosenberg Library at Galveston, joined the Texas Army in 1835 as a captain of infantry. At San Jacinto he served as acting major. Afterwards he was sent to the United States on recruiting service, very likely because he had a presentable uniform, where he enrolled about 230 men. In New Orleans, Allen purchased 496 pair of white drill pants and other items of clothing for the army. He was discharged as a captain on December 2, 1836. In 1838, he was elected mayor of Galveston, serving seven years.[83]

The flag behind Wharton is the 1824 banner used from 1835 through the following year until independence was declared. It was flown over San Antonio after the successful siege of Bexar, according to Ehrenberg, and may have been one of the Texian flags at the Alamo. It was also the flag authorized by the provisional government to be flown by Texas ships sailing under Letters of Marque, according to Mike Green, Reference Archivist of the Texas State Archives.

★   ★   ★

It was at this point that insubordination became such a problem that Houston had some graves dug and posted notices that any who "beat for volunteers" would be tried and shot. That, temporarily at least, put a lid on thoughts of wholesale mutiny.

Mollifying the men slightly was the arrival, despite Houston's orders to restrain further reinforcements, of two small cannons while the army was as the Groce Plantation, a gift from the citizens of Cincinnati, Ohio. The soldiers dubbed them "the twin sisters."

In the meantime, Santa Anna, learning that the Texian president and his cabinet were at Harrisburg, hurried there. He found the city deserted, except for three printers, turning out a last edition of the *Telegraph and Texas Register*. From them he learned Burnet and his cabinet had left only three hours before for the coast near New Washington. He hurried a flying squadron of dragoons after them under Colonel Juan Almonte, the bastard son of famed patriot-priest José María Morelos. Burnet and those with him were pulling away from shore in a rowboat, working the oars vigorously, as Almonte rode up to the water's edge. But in an unusual display of Mexican gallantry,

Almonte ordered his men not to fire, as there was a woman in the boat – Mrs. Burnet.

At Harrisburg, Santa Anna had the city burned, then headed northeast in pursuit of the elusive Houston and all that was left of the Texas Army.

He now knew that Houston had left the Groce Plantation about April 12, still retreating eastward. His determination to catch and overtake Houston's tattered army, coupled with his growing confidence from being victorious so far, plus his utter contempt for the rag-tag enemy led by a alcoholic "general" who was not even respected by his own men, now caused Santa Anna to make reckless mistakes which would be his undoing. His army was weakened by being divided into five separate wings under himself, generals Ganoa, Urrea, Ramírez y Sesma, and Italian-born Vicente Filisola. Most had about 600 to 800 men each, with Filisola having the largest part of the army, approximately 4,000 men. Santa Anna himself, dangerously in advance of all, had a force of only about 750 cavalry and infantry with but a single cannon, "The Golden Standard," a twelve pounder. Perhaps uneasy of his danger, in the unlikely event Houston should turn and fight, but unwilling to slow his pursuit, Santa Anna sent word back to Filisola at his base at Fort Bend to hurry 500 reinforcements to him under his brother-in-law, General Cos.

Much speculation has come down through the years that Houston, an erstwhile protégé of General Andrew Jackson, now the American president, had a secret understanding with Jackson. Houston would, under this possibility, retreat to the Sabine, the more or less border with the United States and sucker the Mexicans into the borderland where the United States Army in Louisiana, under General Edmund Gaines, would then come into the fray and trounce the Mexicans. This would explain perhaps Houston's insistence on continued retreat until the Texas Redlands, where the border was vague, or the American border at the Sabine, was reached. No documentary evidence of this has yet surfaced. But there is some faint circumstantial evidence. For instance, there was an understanding between the Texians and the American government, arranged possibly surreptitiously by Stephen F. Austin, whereby if the Indians of east Texas

menaced white people in the border area, either in Louisiana *or Texas*, Gaines, could put the disorder down with American troops. Using this agreement, Gaines, claiming the Indians were about to take advantage of the distraction of the Texas settlers by their struggle with the Mexicans, actually moved some of his soldiers into Texas and stationed them around Nacogdoches. This would be the trap Houston would lead the Mexicans into, if true, and a clever plan at that. It would vindicate him as a cunning strategist, rather than the posturing, but gutless coward many accused him of being. If it was a *pre-arranged* plan, it had merit. But, unfortunately for Houston, his army was fed up with his continuous retreat and would have none of it. In their eyes he was a "Flashman." The popular fictional Harry Flashman, hero-rogue of a series of rollicking historical adventure stories set all over the British empire and even America in the nineteenth century, though unknown in that period, nevertheless perfectly fitted the image of Sam Houston many held. Flashman, the creation of twentieth century Scottish author George McDonald Fraser, in a series of "diaries," unmasks as a unscrupulous, cowardly, craven womanizer who nevertheless managed to acquire all sorts of military honors which in actuality were deserved by others. President David Burnet called Houston "the prince of humbugs."[84] Jesse Billingsley, who served during the campaign and commanded a company at San Jacinto, voiced the opinion of perhaps the majority of San Jacinto veterans: "Houston is the basest of all men, as he has, by willfully lying, attempted to rob that little band of men of their well earned honors on the battlefield of San Jacinto. He has assumed to himself credit that was due to others."[85]

## The Texas Navy

In the meantime, a vital role was being played by the tiny, four ship Texas Navy purchased by Stephen F. Austin with funds raised in the United States, and some privateers operating under letters of Marque and Reprisal. It was effectively preventing the Mexicans from being reinforced by sea. Had Mexican supply vessels been able to reinforce and supply Santa Anna by this route, far easier than overland, the entire outcome of the campaign might have been drastically different. The schooners, purchased in early 1836, were the 60-ton *Liberty*, the 125-ton *Invincible*, the 125-ton *Independence*, and the 125-ton *Brutus*. President Burnet appointed officers for each ship, naming the senior captain, Charles E. Hawkins of the *Independence*, as Commodore.

★　★　★

*Plate 7 (page 59)*
## CHARLES E. HAWKINS
### Commodore
### Texas Navy

Commodore Charles E. Hawkins was only thirty-six years old when he took command of the first Texas Navy. His first cruise in the *Independence* was from January to March in 1836. He sailed up and down the coast of Mexico, capturing a number of small vessels. The *Independence* then returned to Galveston to guard against an expected invasion by sea. From there it went to New Orleans for repairs, where Hawkins died. He was replaced by Captain George W. Wheelwright. In April the *Independence* sailed for Galveston. On the seventeenth it was engaged by two Mexican warships and, after a four-hour battle was forced to surrender. H.L. Thompson succeeded Hawkins as Commodore.

The uniform in this plate is taken from a replica in the basement of the Texas Memorial Museum in Austin.

The ship behind Commodore Hawkins is the *Independence*, taken from a model in the office of Austin attorney Wayne Gronquist, President of the National Underwater and Marine Agency (NUMA).

The first naval flag authorized by President Burnet was the Mexican tri-color with the numerals "1824" in the center. The flag in this plate is "the Hawkins flag," designed by Commodore Hawkins and used for many years by both the first and second Texas navies. It was intended to deceive the Mexicans because of its similarity to the flag of the United States.

★　★　★

The *Liberty*, under Captain William S. Brown, cruised up and down the coast of Mexico in order to bottle up the Mexican fleet of eight ships. On March 3, he captured the Mexican schooner *Pelicano* near Sisal. Its cargo of flour and foodstuffs was taken to Matagorda. When opened, the flour barrels revealed a contraband cargo of rifles and ammunition intended for the Mexican army. On March 12, near the mouth of the Rio Grande, the *Invincible*, captained by Jeremiah Brown, captured both the *Bravo*, a Mexican supply ship and troop transport, and the *Pocket*, an American ship carrying contraband supplies for the Mexicans from New Orleans. Their cargoes were hurried to Matagorda and sent overland to the Texas Army. The *Liberty*, about the same time, captured the brig *Durango*, also loaded with supplies for Santa Anna.

While most histories credit General Sam Houston and the Texian Army with winning Texas independence in the field, as much or more credit deservedly belonged to the tiny Texas Navy, with only half as many ships as the Mexican Navy, that swept the Texas coast clean of enemy ships carrying supplies for Santa Anna – supplies that fortuitously ended up in Texian hands.

By now the majority of Texian soldiers had been issued the clothing supplies and accoutrements sent by Texas agents in the United States. The average soldier looked something like this.

★　★　★

*Plate 8 (page 60)*
## THE COMMON SOLDIER

So far at least the following supplies had been received and presumably distributed: 867 jackets, 372 pair of pants, 1,550 shirts, 1,284 pair of socks, 351 vests, 2,012 pairs of footgear, 438 canteens, 200 cartridge boxes and belts, 100 knapsacks, 512 muskets (including 72 with bayonets), plus 100 carbines and 100 pistols, 60 cavalry swords and 75 sabres. Strength of the army ran from a high of 1,500 on the Colorado to a low of 500 at the Groce Plantation, then up to 783 or so at San Jacinto. So, considering that the New Orleans Greys, Alabama Red Rovers, Newport Kentucky Rifles, and the U.S. Army regulars were in their own uniforms, the balance of the rank and file were outfitted more or less uniformly with these components.

The jackets were roundabouts, a short waist-length jacket popular with civilians and seamen alike. It was not unlike the "Ike jacket" of World War II. It came in two styles, single breasted or double breasted. The purchases do not indicate which style the Texas agents in the United States supplied, perhaps both, as there was more than one shipment. While color was never specified, it was usually white. The pants were usually white also, usually made of sailcloth. Most of the shirts were probably white also, though some were brown, red flannel, or twilled gingham or twilled checks. The footgear was almost all brogans (a heavy work shoe), the majority kip (untanned leather), others russet.

The soldier holds a Kentucky-Pennsylvania type long rifle. These rifles were far more accurate than the smoothbore muskets of the Mexicans, but were slower to load.

The powder horn, gourd canteen, and hat are in the Fort Bend County Museum, Fort Bend, Texas. The hat belonged to C.C. Dyer, one of Austin's original "old three-hundred" colonists.

Behind the soldier is Captain Brown's "Flag of the Bloody Sword." Designed by Captain William Brown, it was first unfurled at Goliad on December 20, 1835 when the Goliad Declaration of Independence was adopted before that of the Council in March of 1836. It was one of the ten Texian battle flags of the revolution.

In the background is the steamboat *Yellow Stone*. The *Yellow Stone*, owned by Toby and Brother Company, later Texas agents in New Orleans, had a significant role in the Texas Revolution. On its first trip to Texas in December of 1835, it brought forty-seven members of the Mobile Greys. It was tied up at Groce's Landing when the retreating Texas Army arrived on March 31. General Houston impressed it into service to ferry the army across the Brazos. It then steamed downstream, picking up refugees in the Runaway Scrape. At Fort Bend it passed so close to Mexican soldiers on the bank that one of the Mexicans attempted, unsuccessfully, to lasso one of its two stacks. After San Jacinto, it brought the Texian government back from Galveston island and served other assignments for the interim government. The ship's bell is now in the Alamo Museum.

★　　★　　★

## The Fork in the Road

As the retreating Texians neared the fork in the road and the crucial decision had to be made whether to continue on towards the American border at the Sabine or hook southward to the right towards Harrisburg to meet the Mexicans, Houston and his army were themselves at the fork in the road in their relationship with each other. The night before the fork in the road was to be reached the Texian camp was in a state of high excitement. The Secretary of War, Rusk, and most of the officers were pressuring the Commander-in-Chief to take the south fork – the Harrisburg road – for the confrontation they desired with the Mexican Dictator, whose position had been learned from captured dispatches.[86] This was also the obvious will of the rank and file. Houston was still reluctant. Some expected him to desert that night.[87]

On April 17, the van reached the crucial fork in the road. As yet no order had been received as to which route to take, according to several contemporary accounts. Houston was lagging behind. Standing at the gate of his property at the crossroads was a Mr. Roberts, according to Dr. Labadie. When Labadie and others inquired which fork was the Harrisburg road, Roberts, in a loud, clear voice announced with a wave of his hand, "That right hand road will take you to Harrisburg just as straight as a compass!" At once a shout went up, "To the right, boys, to the right!" The musicians then turned down the Harrisburg road, with the rest of the army following behind jubilantly.[88] If Houston had not made up his mind by then, the decision was made for him by his army. "We compelled Old Sam to take the road to Harrisburg," chortled Amasa Turner, captain of Company B, Burleson's regiment of infantry.[89]

Confirming that Houston had planned to take the other road was the arrival of Mrs. Pamela Mann, a formidable woman who turned up to reclaim her yoke of oxen, until now pulling one of the cannon. She let Houston know in no uncertain terms that he had violated his assurance to her that the borrowed oxen were to go to the Trinity. Now that he had changed course, she demanded them back. And, despite his protest that they were vital, the pistol-toting Mrs. Mann unhitched them and made off with them.[90]

The two armies were now on a collision course.

Now Rusk began to take a more assertive role. Objecting to a campsite chosen by Houston as inappropriate, he cajoled the general into moving to a better position more or less hidden in a grove of trees backed up against Buffalo Bayou. Ahead of them was a clear area of about a mile with waist high grass, which would give a clean view of the Mexicans when they approached.

At this point Santa Anna was not aware that the Texas Army had turned and was advancing towards him. He was confident Houston was still intent on retreating to the Redlands and probably safety in the United States. He was hurrying to overtake the tiny Texas Army to deliver the final blow, unaware that they were dead ahead – *waiting for him.*

On April 20, Santa Anna's vanguard was sighted coming across the open field in front of the Texan position. They were still quite oblivious to the fact that the Texians, concealed in their woods, were now only a mile or so distant.

Houston, restless and uneasy, according to Labadie, paced back and forth. He had the twin sisters hauled out and positioned. "Moreland, are you ready?" he asked Isaac N. Moreland, who was then in charge of the artillery. Moreland objected that the range was too far. "Clear the guns and fire," Houston insisted. The shot fell harmlessly short. All that had been accomplished was the loss or surprise.[91]

Santa Anna, amazed that he had found the Texians, and more so that they had artillery, reacted by bringing up his only artillery piece, the Golden Standard, a 12-pounder. Sidney Sherman, eager for glory, pestered Houston to let him take some mounted men to attempt to capture the Mexican's only field piece. Houston suspected, not without good reason, that Sherman hoped to bring on a general engagement, but reluctantly agreed. With about sixty horsemen Sherman sallied forth, but the Mexicans withdrew. Mexican dragoons and infantry then hurried forward to cut off Sherman's horsemen. In the resultant melee the Texians fared badly. They had to dismount to fire and reload their long rifles. In the skirmish, Secretary of War Rusk was cut off and would have come to mishap but for the courageous act of a relatively new recruit, with the romantic name of Mirabeau Buonaparte Lamar. Lamar charged his sturdy stallion into a Mexican horseman, knocking him aside and creating a gap through which Rusk escaped. As the Texians retreated one youngster, Walter P. Lane, later to be a Confederate general, was unhorsed and fleeing afoot, about to be run down by Mexican lancers. Seeing Lane's predicament, Lamar again wheeled about to the rescue. He interposed his horse between Lane and the Lancers, dropping one with his pistol. This gave another mounted Texian, Captain Henry Karnes, time to pick up the wounded Lane and skedaddle with him. Admiring this act of bravado, the Mexican dragoons pulled up short and applauded the daring rescuers. Lamar, who from his gallantry this day was promoted to colonel, and who later became vice president and then President of Texas, faced the Mexicans and gave a gallant bow.[97]

In the meantime, Jesse Billingsley, seeing the distress of the horsemen and angered that Houston had reneged on the infantry support promised if they experienced difficulties, hurried his company of infantry to their aid. The first regiment of infantry, under Edward Burleson, who detested Houston, joined Billingsley's company. As they passed in front of a furious Sam Houston, the general demanded they countermarch. They ignored their Commander-in-Chief. With amusement, Billingsley recalled, "This order the men treated with derision, requesting him to countermarch himself, if he desired it, and steadily held on their way to the support of Colonel Sherman, and succeeded in driving the enemy back behind their breastworks."[93]

*Was Jesse Billingsley uniformed?* One descendant says *yes*, he wore a uniform and that *it is still extant*. But there is a family feud over the uniform. According to this descendant, it is kept in a barn by an elderly lady who has threatened that if any relative from the other faction tries to get the uniform she will burn the barn. Efforts to contact her to include it in this book met with a firm rebuff from her daughter, who denied access to her mother or that the uniform exists. Some versions about the uniform suggest it may have belonged to Jesse Billingsley's father, Rueben, who wore it in the War of 1812, and Jesse wore his father's uniform and sword at San Jacinto; or that the mysterious uniform in the barn (presuming there is such a uniform) is a post-revolution militia uniform that belonged to a son of Jesse Billingsley, Jeptha, or a grandson, Rueben. In the barn (presuming the barn actually exists) is also the sword, according to my source.

## San Jacinto

April 21, 1836, everyone in the Texian ranks was eager to fight – all except their commander it appeared. The men rose early with reveille at 4 a.m. They paraded, awaiting orders, according to Labadie. But the only order from their Commander-in-Chief was that he was not to be disturbed before 8 a.m. He was sleeping.

When Houston awoke he received a nasty surprise. Coming across Vince's Bridge was General Cos with the 500 reinforcements Santa Anna had requested. They had force marched all night. Until now the two sides were more or less even in strength. Now Santa Anna possessed a more or less two-to-one advantage. If further reinforcements arrived from Filisola or other of the Mexican columns, the Texians had no chance at all.

Houston lamely tried to pass off the Mexican reinforcement as "only a sham – no reinforcement."[94] His men were not deceived. Later, when asked by the captured Santa Anna why he had allowed Cos' men to slip through, Houston offered this explanation, "I didn't want to take two bites from one cherry."[95] It was a glib, but unconvincing cover for a serious mistake.

At this point Houston had 783 bitter die-hards left. Santa Anna now had at least 1,250, perhaps more.

Somewhat earlier, the Texians had received a modest reinforcement themselves as two uniformed companies from the United States mysteriously appeared in their ranks. These were U.S. Army regulars.

★ ★ ★

*Plate 9 (page 61)*
## AMERICAN ARMY VOLUNTEERS

The United States regulars who fought at San Jacinto were garrison troops from Louisiana. That there was collusion between their commander, General Edmund P. Gaines and perhaps even the President of the United States, Houston's mentor Andrew Jackson, and the Texians was virtually a certainty. In a letter dated April 15, 1836, from Stephen F. Austin to the American President, his cabinet, and certain influential congressmen, Austin urged: "let the war in Texas become a national war, above board … it is now a national war sub rosa."[96] Contributing to the suspicion of collusion is that the American soldiers who went over to Texas were listed officially as "deserters" – but on their return none were ever tried for desertion.

The uniformed American soldiers were placed under the command of Lieutenant Colonel Henry Millard of the Texas regulars. They were classed as regulars in the Texas Army, also, but with two distinctions: their officers were appointed, not elected, and they received a larger land bounty for their services.

In the illustration the soldier wears the American army field uniform of the period with his U.S. insignia "disguised with buckskin accessories."[97] A buckskin flap, for instance, covers the U.S. brass insignia plate on his cartridge box. He has also removed the U.S. brass circular belt plate with its American eagle from one of his cross belts. Whether or not the showy epaulets would actually have been worn in battle might be questioned, but they were regulation. And it was an age of flashy uniforms. At Goliad, for instance, the Mexicans had dressed in their parade uniforms to perform the executions. The American Army, which in Louisiana was primarily to keep a watchful eye on the Indians on both sides of the border with Texas, in those days well knew the value of dressy uniforms to awe the Indians, according to artist-historian Randy Steffen.[98]

Which hat the American soldier wore then might also be questioned. Some contend it was the black leather collapsible "hogkiller" monstrosity, then regulation. However it was government policy to first use up existing supplies before replacing them with newly regulated items. Whatever else garrisons in other parts of the country might have been wearing in the 1830s, the research of military artist-historian Fritz Kredel show the soft cap still being worn at the time of the Texas Revolution and, more specifically, that of the late artist-historian Joseph Hefter, shows the soft cloth cap as being worn by the Louisiana garrison troops, not the leather "hogkiller."[99]

The flag behind the American soldier is the San Jacinto flag brought by the Kentucky volunteers under Sidney Sherman, the only flag carried by the Texans in the final battle.

★   ★   ★

Until now Sam Houston had consulted no one, held no councils. But now his officers were insistent in demanding a council. Houston acceded. Exactly what transpired during that conference is a matter of dispute.

The officers wanted to fight. But they were in disagreements as to whether it was wiser to remain in their favorable position for the Mexicans to attack them, or to attack the Mexicans. Houston cautioned that, in either case, the Texans were "raw militia" with none but himself having ever been in a "general engagement," whereas the Mexicans were "well-disciplined regulars."[100] Instead, he proposed building a portable bridge upon which to escape, a proposal which met with universal disdain.[101] The conference broke up in indecision, divided on whether to await a Mexican attack or attack themselves. None, however, wanted any further retreat.

When word spread about the encampment of Houston's plan for a portable bridge, it was met with derision. "The men said they would not work to build a bridge," remembered Amasa Turner, "but would go out and whip the Mexicans while Old Sam built his bridge."[102]

This was reinforced by Dr. Labadie, who said, "An immediate hand-to-hand fight was the desire of all the men."[103]

All day Colonel John Wharton had moved about the camp agitating the restless soldiers. "Boys, there is no other word today but <u>fight! Fight</u>!" adding, "the enemy has thousands that can and will concentrate at this point within the next few days … (we) have no reasonable ex-

pectation of a stronger force … The enemy must be fought <u>today</u>, lest tomorrow prove too late."[104] He also agitated Houston. "Sir, the men are willing and ready and anxious to meet the enemy," according to Captain Amasa Turner. Turner, who was present, said, "Old Sam said the officers will not fight – they have so decided in council this day. Wharton said they would and the men too and '*unless you order otherwise I will order the army to form for battle.*'"[105]

Then, according to several accounts, an exasperated Houston replied, "Fight then and be damned."[106]

Houston admirers have a very different version. According to biographies written by his supporters, Sam Houston arose that morning confident, determined that this was the day to do battle, exclaiming, "the sun of Austerlitz* has risen again." He went about the encampment during the morning visiting each mess, conducting his own poll concerning their willingness to fight. Receiving an overwhelming affirmative response, he told the Texians, "Very well, get your dinners and I will lead you into the fight and if you whip them every one of you shall be a captain."[107] Late in the afternoon, he secretly sent his best scout, Erastus ("Deaf") Smith, to destroy Vince's Bridge, over which more Mexican reinforcements might come. Without the floating bridge, destruction of Vince's Bridge also cut off the Texans only escape route.

This could be questioned as another serious error by Houston, though as things turned out it fortunately didn't matter. But most strategists would argue that it is never wise to back yourself into a corner with no means of retreat. Cortes had done this when he burned his ships at Veracruz, but he was motivated by distrust of the resolve of his men. Whether this was also Houston's motive can only be guessed.

There was now no recourse for either army but to fight. Santa Anna had chosen his campsite poorly, hemmed in mostly by water and the Texians. Houston's choice was even worse. While a good defensive position, he now had water on three sides and the Mexicans in front.

_____

*One of Napoleon's greatest victories.

Wharton, according to Labadie, was now going about the camp exuberantly proclaiming that the order to fight had been given at last.[108] It was now past three in the afternoon, unusually late to begin a battle. But the army assembled eagerly. Even as the Texians were now forming up for battle, Houston was hesitant, according to Mirabeau B. Lamar, the new colonel of cavalry. "Houston came to me and said, 'Colonel Lamar, do you really think we ought to fight?'"[109]

Having decided that by now the Texians weren't going to attack, at least this day, the Mexicans were relaxing. There were no lookouts that the Texians could discern. Cos' men, exhausted by their overnight march were sleeping. Most of Santa Anna's infantry, exhausted from spending most of the night constructing a makeshift barricade, were also asleep. Even the dictator himself was having a late siesta in his tent.* The cavalry was riding their horses bareback to and from the water. The Mexicans were literally *caught napping*.

Whether or not he was making a virtue of necessity, Houston, after assigning each unit its place in the coming battle, now mounted a magnificent white stallion named Saracen, acquired from Groce while at his plantation. There are several descriptions of the formation, but this seems the most reliable:

on the left Sherman with his uniformed Kentuckians, Burleson at the head of the Texas regulars (one company of which was at least partially uniformed, as we shall discover later), the twin sisters commanded by George Hockley, more infantry under Secretary of War Rusk, Henry Millard at the head of the uniformed United States infantry (two companies), and at the far right the cavalry under the newly promoted Lamar. The flag probably was with the Kentuckians, though a Mexican' officer's description places it in the center.

---

*Texas folklore has it that he was dallying amorously with a mulatto slave woman, Emily Morgan, found at the Groce Plantation. Dubbed "the Yellow Rose of Texas," she supposedly was purposely distracting the dictator to help the Texians. There is no truth to this popular yarn.

## Remember the Alamo! Remember Goliad!

The determined little band now totaled 783; with about thirty-three left in camp, some as guards, some sick; 750 were in battle array. Houston and Rusk gave short speeches, and the battle cry "*Remember the Alamo! Remember Goliad!*" Then the last hope of Texas moved forward to their date with destiny. It was now 4:30 in the afternoon.

At first they advanced in a single file, Indian style. Then they spread out. Houston dressed the line. As they proceeded, the artillerymen pulling their tiny cannons by ropes, Houston constantly cautioned them to proceed as silently as possible and to hold their fire. *Surprise would be everything*.

The first inkling the Mexicans had of the Texian advance was when a bugler summoned Colonel Pedro Delgado with a warning that the enemy was approaching. Delgado, hardly able to believe what he had heard, climbed atop an ammunition box to see for himself. The mile or so of high grass between the two positions partially concealed the silently approaching Texians, Houston on his beautiful white stallion in the lead. They were now within two hundred yards of the Mexican breastworks, a flimsy affair of boxes and baggage, and in the act of turning around their two cannons and positioning them, Delgado, stunned, observed:

I saw their formation was a mere line of one rank, and very extended. In their center was the Texas flag; on both wings they had two light cannons, well manned. Their cavalry was opposite our front, overlapping our left. In this disposition, yelling furiously, with a brisk fire of grape, muskets and rifles, they advanced resolutely upon our camp. There the utmost confusion prevailed.[110]

The four-piece Texian band, fifes and a drum, began to play. As their cannons roared, cavalry and infantry – everyone but the sick and camp guard – rushed forward behind the flag with its LIBERTY OR DEATH motto as it and the ball glove took the breeze. They shouted a fearful battle cry: "*Remember the Alamo! Remember Goliad!*"

Halfway to the enemy breastworks Houston ordered a halt and commanded the men to fire. But the frontier army disobeyed. They reckoned the distance too far for effective fire. "Fire away! God damn you, fire! Aren't you going to fire at all?" Houston roared.[111] In this moment of confusion the Secretary of War, colonel Rusk, at the top of his voice shouted a countermand, "If we stop we are cut to pieces. Don't stop – go ahead – give them hell!"[112] The men obeyed Rusk, not Houston. Disobeying their Commander-in-Chief probably saved the Texians, for their ongoing rush prevented the Mexicans from firing the Golden Standard effectively and rallying. At this point one of the twin sisters had to cease firing, according to one of the gunners, Ben McCulloch, because Houston was prancing his horse right in front of the cannon.[113] "I thought it very strange for him to be there for it was not the place for a sane general to be," Amasa Turner opinioned, "No one good reason could be given for his being there."[114]

About this time, when the Texians were about sixty yards from the barricade, Deaf Smith came thundering along the line on a lathered horse shouting, "Vince's Bridge is down! Fight for your lives! Vince's Bridge is down!"[115] At forty yards Houston's horse, Saracen, went down, hit by multiple bullets. At the barricade, the Texians poured over, firing and reloading, though some, instead of reloading, used their rifles as clubs on the disorganized Mexicans. After an initial hasty resistance at the barricade, most of the Mexicans, particularly those who hadn't even been able to unstack their muskets, became panic-stricken and took flight. On both sides discipline broke down completely and it was every man for himself.

"Once the Mexican soldier panics," Colonel Delgado admitted ruefully, "there is no stopping him."[116] Among the first of the Mexicans to make a getaway was Santa Anna himself, the self-styled "Napoleon of the West." Mounting the finest horse, a black stallion also from Groce's plantation, he speedily outdistanced the other fugitives. A number of his staff were right behind him. Leaderless, the Mexicans, except for scattered pockets of resistance, fled in all directions. Many, unable to swim, bunched up at waterways, where they were cut down by

the Texians' well-aimed rifles, or brained with the butt end of rifles and, not infrequently, fell to the Texians' well-honed Bowie knives. Only the United States regulars and one company of Burleson's regiment had bayonets (the company that was more or less uniformed).

Over and over sounded the unnerving battle cry, "*Remember the Alamo! Remember Goliad!*" Even those Mexicans who didn't speak English understood its meaning clearly. Some begged for their lives, shrieking, "*Me no Alamo! Me no Goliad!*"[117] Blatant lies that did them little good. Also unhelpful were pleas of "*No me mata, Soldades God Damnes!*" The Mexicans had observed over the course of the campaign that the Texians were forever shouting "God Damn!" They assumed it was a battle cry of sorts. Thus their nickname for the Texians was the *God Damn Soldiers*. To those Texians who understood Spanish, and many did, it was highly insulting.

All of the pent up frustration and fury from the defeats at the Alamo and Goliad, and the unpardonable massacre there of the prisoners, and the long galling retreat now gave vent to unrestrained revenge. Efforts of some of the Texian officers to restrain their men were, for the most part, futile. Santa Anna had sounded the *Deguello* at the Alamo and only the day before during the skirmish over the Golden Standard. This sinister bugle call signaled *no quarter* – no prisoners to be taken – a holdover from the wars with the Moors long ago in Spain. The Texians were well aware of its merciless meaning.

Houston mounted a runaway Mexican cavalry horse caught by an aide, and rejoined the fight, slashing at fleeing Mexicans with his sabre. But, according to Amasa Turner, he hung back, not passing the Mexican camp.[118] As the struggle passed beyond the camp, Rusk and Wharton, the latter described later as "the keenest blade at San Jacinto,"[119] had now usurped Houston's authority and were exercising such direction as they could over the virtually out-of-control Texians.

Not all of the Mexicans behaved cowardly. General Manuel Fernandez Castrillón, a seasoned veteran of many campaigns, unable to rally his command and seeing that all was lost, stood fast, arms folded and facing the enemy. "I have been in forty battles and never showed my back," he said defiantly in Spanish, "I am too old to do it now." Rusk, filled with admiration, attempted to spare him. "Don't shoot him," he pleaded, "Don't shoot him!" knocking up several rifles aimed at the old soldier. But others getting past Rusk riddled the brave old Castillian aristocrat.[120]

One of the oldest Texians was "Uncle Jimmy" Curtis, 64. His son-in-law, Washington Cottle, whom he had never gotten along with, had died at the Alamo, a member of the Gonzales contingent. At San Jacinto Uncle Jimmy was having a fine time drinking whiskey and terrorizing and killing Mexicans. He had his special battle cry: "Remember *Wash Cottle*!" Someone pointed out to him that he had never liked Wash Cottle. "The Mexicans don't know that," laughed Uncle Jimmy.[121]

In another of his questionable acts, Houston, now on his third horse and with a bullet in his left ankle,* called for retreat to be sounded on the drum. None obeyed. "Parade, men, parade!" he commanded futilely. "Halt! Glory enough has been gained this day, and blood enough has been shed … Gentlemen! Gentlemen! Gentlemen! I applaud your bravery, but damn your manners."[122]

Again, Rusk countermanded him. "Your order, general, cannot be obeyed … No, it is not enough while the enemy is in sight."[123]

"Have I a friend in this world?" Houston asked bitterly.[124] He was fearful that other Mexican reinforcements might arrive while the Texians were in total disorganization. In his state of nerves, he thought that had actually happened when a column of Mexican prisoners was seen approaching from about a half mile away, guarded by Texians. Thinking they were Filisola's men he threw up his hands in despair, crying "All is lost! All is lost! My God, all is lost!"[125]

When Colonel Wharton whispered something to him Houston bristled resentfully. "Colonel Wharton, you have commanded long enough: damn you, go about your business."[126] Followed by some of his staff, he then rode back to the Texian bivouac. Amasa Turner, whose company had been designated to guard the Mexican camp to prevent looting, said, "at the time he left he appeared the

most distressed crazy creature I ever saw. He did not appear to have one particle of sense left."[127]

The Texians pressed their advantage until nightfall. This was wise because had other Mexican forces arrived, those of Ramírez y Sesma, Ganoa, Urrea, or Filisola, the latter alone having more than 4,000, they could have turned the tide of battle.

The entire engagement took only about eighteen minutes. It was in truth won by its spunky rank and file, not by its general. The results were astounding. Mexican dead numbered 630. Captured were 600, of whom 208 were wounded. Few escaped. The Texians casualties were two killed, twenty-three wounded, of whom six later died.

## Santa Anna Captured

Though San Jacinto was a magnificent victory, it would not have ended the war except for the fortunate capture of Santa Anna. He was taken the next day by a five-man patrol led by one of the uniformed Kentucky volunteers, James A. Sylvester, the flag bearer, while searching for Mexican stragglers. The wily dictator, to save his own skin, made a hasty deal with the Texas leaders. First came an armistice agreement, later two peace treaties, one public, and one private. Emissaries were sent to General Vicente Filisola, the senior Mexican officer in the field, as soon as the armistice was signed, to apprise him of it.

There are good descriptions of a couple of the volunteers at San Jacinto, particularly Colonel Edward Burleson and Sergeant Moses Austin Bryan.

★  ★  ★

*Plate 10 (page 62)*
## COLONEL EDWARD BURLESON

There are two descriptions of Colonel Edward Burleson at San Jacinto, both similar. His grandson, Albert Sidney Burleson, remembered: he was blond, with steel blue eyes, height five feet eleven inches, weighing about 180 pounds. He was smooth-shaven, wore a light blue Eton jacket and a small brown hat with a very narrow brim with a flat Quaker crown. A dark red sash held up his corduroy trousers. He did not have a sword, but carried two pistols,

---

*That it was a copper ball created some suspicion it came from one of his own men.

one carried in its holster on the horn of his saddle, the other he carried in his hand. He rode a sorrel horse. A granddaughter, Emma Kyle Burleson, said that instead of a uniform he wore a short Eton jacket and snuff-colored trousers, a small rimmed black hat and did not use or carry a sword.[128]

Burleson was a formidable Indian fighter and ranger in pre-revolutionary Texas and long after during the Republic and statehood. During the campaign, he developed an intense contempt for Sam Houston.

He was later a general during the Republic of Texas and was vice president under President Mirabeau B. Lamar. He ran for president against Anson Jones in 1844, claiming as his main qualification that he "had killed more Mexicans and Indians than any other Texan,"[129] but lost to Houston's protégé.

Behind him is shown the "Come And Take It" flag and the diminutive "Come And Take It" cannon over which the revolution began.*

★   ★   ★

*Plate 11 (page 63)*
## SERGEANT MOSES AUSTIN BRYAN

Moses Austin Bryan, a nephew of Stephen F. Austin, was an eighteen year old sergeant during the battle of San Jacinto. He is shown here with a long arm, but during the battle he used a shotgun for the close up fighting. After firing his shotgun only about four times, he became disgusted by the carnage and spent the rest of the battle trying unsuccessfully to save the lives of Mexicans who wanted to surrender. After the battle he helped translate for the conversation between Houston and Santa Anna until Texas interim Vice President Lorenzo de Zavala and

Santa Anna's aide Colonel Juan Almonte, who had been educated in the United States and spoke perfect English, took over.

Here Bryan is wearing a "claw-hammer" tail coat that had belonged to his uncle, a Mexican sombrero and high-topped leather moccasins.

Behind him is the flag of the Harrisburg Volunteers. Made by Sarah Rudolph Dodson it went with the Harrisburg Volunteers to the relief of the Gonzales colonists when they defied the Mexicans over the Come and Take It cannon, and was with them at the siege of Bexar.

The two cannon in the background are the "twin sisters," the two small 6-pounders donated by the citizens of Cincinnati, Ohio. The sisters played a decisive role in the battle of San Jacinto. They remained in the arsenal of the Republic of Texas and were later in Confederate service. They were surrendered to the federals at Houston, Texas along with other Confederate ordnance at the end of the Civil War. But supposedly certain Texana sentimentalists ferreted them out of the ordnance depot and surreptitiously buried them, intending to dig them up later and restore them to a suitable place of honor. Unfortunately, so the story goes, in the meantime someone built a building on the site or paved a road over it. Whatever the case, their whereabouts are now unknown. Replicas of them are on display at Camp Mabry, headquarters of the Texas National Guard, Austin, Texas.

★   ★   ★

There were several mentions of the uniforms being in the battle of San Jacinto. From the descriptions of their being Texas Regulars with bayonets, they were probably the United States Army volunteers, perhaps the Newport Rifles, or both. However, they might been from the company of Captain Henry Teal that was with Burleson's Texas Regulars. Teal and two of his men, the later in uniforms, are mentioned in the diary of a Mexican officer, José de la Peña, who was with Filisola when the Texian emissaries arrived at his camp with the Santa Anna surrender documents and instructions from the captured dictator.

---

*The Come and Take It cannon, when discarded on the march to San Antonio, was buried near Sandies Creek on the road between Gonzales and San Antonio. Its location was forgotten. In 1936, during the Texas Centennial year, it was washed up by a flood. A rural mail carrier found it and took it to the Gonzales Post Office, where it rested in the basement for thirty years, its identity unsuspected. When the post office was moved it disappeared. Later it was acquired by Dr. Pat Wagner of Shiner, who by scientific tests proved beyond doubt that it was the Gonzales "Come and Take It" cannon. The original cannon is in the Gonzales Memorial Museum, Gonzales, Texas. A replica is on loan to the Bob Bullock Texas History Museum, Austin, Texas.

## Uniforms of Teal's Company

"Two Texas soldiers and three other persons appeared whose presence excited enthusiasm and caused some to believe the enemy was advancing, and they repaired to await them. In fact, these were Benjamin F. Smith, McIntyre and Henry Teal, who called themselves colonel, major, and captain in the Texas Army; and who brought the agreement entered into. The two orderlies with them are the first uniformed soldiers we have seen up to now, which has caused some amazement among our men."[130] Actually Teal was uniformed as well.

The uniforms of Teal and his two "orderlies" are mentioned again in an account by Reuben Marmaduke Potter of the mission of Captains Teal and Henry Karnes to Urrea in Matamoros, sanctioned by Filisola, to negotiate the freedom of Texians held prisoner there. In his letter to H.A. McArdle, the artist who painted the epic oils of the Alamo and San Jacinto which now hang in the Texas capitol, Potter, who had been an agent for a commercial house in Matamoros, described Teal as "a captain of regular infantry." He described the two "orderlies" who accompanied Teal and Karnes as "soldiers of Teal's company."[131] With them also was a French resident of Texas, Victor Loupé, who acted as interpreter.

Potter was the first to greet them on their arrival. He described the officers as having shoulder straps indicating their rank, and the uniforms of the two soldiers as "rather ungainly" and "baggy."[132] This raises the suspicion that these were strictly homemade Texian uniforms, as the American uniforms of the day were trim. While Potter described both officers as having shoulder straps he also made the contradictory statement that "Karnes, not being a regular, had no uniform."[133] But Potter gives no clue as to the color or details of the three uniforms that would enable us to form an idea of exactly what they looked like. Perhaps the only likely surmise is that they were gray, as prescribed by the convention in March. Teal formed his company of about forty men, after receiving his commission from the convention. They had reported to Houston at Gonzales and were with him at San Jacinto.[134]

After receiving their credentials, Urrea first demanded they doff their uniforms, saying they angered the Mexicans. Next he stalled them. Unwilling to accept the deal made by the captive dictator, he was planning a re-invasion of Texas, and didn't want them to carry back an alarm to alert the Texians. While more or less captives, though with the run of the city, Teal and Karnes managed to sneak out a warning to Houston concealed in the hollow handle of a whip. Some time in September, they managed to escape, aided by Potter and some sympathetic Americans. The conspirators sent their belongings across the river to their hiding place. Teal's uniform and sword, however were not included, because of the antagonism they would cause if discovered. But Teal wouldn't leave without his uniform and sword, so these were finally sneaked out to him. They then left to rejoin the army.[135]

## Uniformed Generals

Bustling about in the United States during the revolution were two gentlemen claiming the title of general, Thomas Jefferson Chambers and Felix Huston (no relation to Sam Houston), who were raising money and men, purchasing arms and uniforms. Chambers received his title as Major General of the Army of the Reserve from the provisional government on his promise to recruit and outfit soldier-emigrants from the United States at his own expense. The source of Huston's title is unclear. Chambers was a long-time Texian. Huston was an adventurer originally from Kentucky, more lately from Mississippi. Neither had previous military experience, and neither was in any battle of the revolution. Among their first acts, however, was to outfit themselves with uniforms.

Chamber's coat, belt, and sword may be seen displayed in the San Jacinto Monument.

★　★　★

*Plate 12 (page 64)*
## THOMAS JEFFERSON CHAMBERS
### Major General of the Army of the Reserve

Chambers, in addition to uniforming himself, bought clothing and cavalry helmets for the Texas Army at his own expense. Exactly how many men he outfitted is uncertain. This particular coat has had an unusual *history in hiding*. It was first donated to the Rosenberg Library in Galveston, but languished in storage, never displayed. After some years it was transferred to the San Jacinto Monument as presumably a more suitable repository for it. There it also remained in storage, and was forgotten.

When preparing my book *Uniforms of the Republic of Texas* I was advised by Brigadier General Jay A. Matthews, Jr. that Chamber's uniform, in remarkably good condition, was at the Monument, but in storage. When I inquired about it, however, I received a curious answer, which didn't say yes or no. When preparing this book I journeyed again to the monument in search of items pertaining to the revolution and – lo and behold – there was Chambers' coat which he designed and wore in the revolutionary period, and perhaps into the Republic of Texas era, as his commission carried over in the Army of the Republic.

The explanation received from officials at the monument was that at one point they received a grant form the Daughters of the Republic of Texas, which they used to inventory stored items. During the inventory the coat was discovered (the belt and sword had already been on exhibit) and put on display. There is also an epaulet, not attached to the coat, which may have been from a later uniform during the republic years. There is also an oil portrait of Chambers displayed, but in civilian clothes.

Behind General Chambers is the flag of the San Felipe Volunteers. It was made by the ladies of San Felipe for the company of Captain Moseley Baker. The original design had been suggested by Stephen F. Austin to be the national flag of Texas. At the upper left it had a British Union Jack and below it a green field with the lone star of Texas. To the right it had thirteen red and white stripes like the United States flag. On the white stripes were the words OUR COUNTRY'S RIGHTS OR DEATH.[136]

★　★　★

Felix Huston claimed to have spent forty thousand dollars (a tremendous sum in those days) uniforming and equipping 500 emigrants, who arrived after the fighting was over. His self-designed uniform is shown in *Uniforms of the Republic of Texas*, since his real service was mainly

during the Republic of Texas. The cut and color of the uniforms of the men he outfitted was unspecified. Again, most probably it was the gray prescribed by the convention in March. These would most likely have been similar to the uniform of Travis shown in Plate 4, but with a shell jacket instead of a tail coat, and with white metal buttons for infantry, instead of the yellow buttons, which were for cavalry.

On May 13, the Virginia gentleman Colonel William Fairfax Gray encountered Huston at Marion, Texas: "there is General Felix Huston, dressed *a la militaire*. Tall and well-made, rather slender. Bearing of a proud, ambitious man, evidently making an effort to be free and easy, so as to win popular favor."[137]

Earlier, in New Orleans, Colonel Gray had observed some of the Texian agents recruiting. He made this entry in his diary: "Find a number of Texans, officers and others, raising troops, Green, Conrad, Thornton, etc. They fill the bar rooms of the public houses, and make too much display of uniforms, etc."[138] Exactly what these uniforms looked like, or whether there was any uniformity to them, or whether they were patterned after what was prescribed by the Convention in March or were imaginatively self-created is unknown. It is possible that some of the 2,000 gray uniforms ordered by the Convention had arrived by now.

## More Supplies Ordered

Between the April victory at San Jacinto and the creation of the Republic of Texas in early October, the army swelled and efforts to provide it with arms and uniforms increased accordingly.

A week after the battle Commissary General Forbes purchase in New Orleans from Colonel James Powers for use of the Texas Army: 100 pair duck pantaloons; 365 cotton shirts; 14 pair white woolen (illegible).[139]

A May 15 list from General John Forbes to Secretary of War Rusk of "sundries" required for "immediate use" of the army included: 1,000 caps; 1,000 leather stocks; 1,000 cotton duck roundabouts; 1,500 cotton duck pantaloons; 1,000 pair socks; 2,000 pair shoes assorted; 500 pair Duffield blankets; 1,000 haversacks; 1,000 knapsacks; 10 gross pint tin cups; 5 gross tin canteens; 100

gross rifles; 150 pair pistols and holsters (probably for the cavalry); 200 swords, belts, and other accessories for cavalry; 200 short Yagers for cavalry; *300 yards of gray cloth for officers uniforms and gold lace for trimming.*[140] This last item is especially interesting. For, combined with later requests for *gray thread*, and for tailors to be assigned to make uniforms, it shows that though Texas looked mainly to the United States for its needs in military clothing, it now intended to make some of it within Texas.

On June 1, Robert Triplett, Texas general agent in New Orleans, acknowledged receipt of $330 to cover an order from Robert Potter, recently appointed commander of the port of Galveston for uniforms, etc. These were for the ships Invincible, Brutus, and Liberty, and possibly for Navy Yard personnel.[141]

On June 19, as he shopped about the United States, Chambers wrote from Nashville, Tennessee to a Colonel Ira Lewis regarding uniforms: " please procure the articles in the enclosed lists, and according to their models and descriptions. The articles that cannot be had ready-made you will please have manufactured immediately."[142]

June 23, President Burnet sent to Thomas Toby & Brother, who had now replaced Triplett as Texas agent, a list of supplies required for the army. Clothing included: 2,000 common cotton shirts stout; 2,000 pair common summer pantaloons stout; 1,000 round jackets; 1,000 pair coarse shoes; 1,000 cartridge boxes and belts; 1,000 bayonet belts and scabbards; 200 cavalry sabers (such as used by the U.S. Dragoons); 200 pair horsemens pistols with holsters for same. The balance of the order was for rifle and musket flints, bullets, muskets, bayonets, and twenty barrels of whiskey.[143]

The president on July 8 expressed relief to Major General Mirabeau B. Lamar, now Commander-in-Chief of the army, that Lamar had found "even a small supply of clothing for the army," adding, "We have two large orders in New Orleans for clothing and still hope a portion of them will soon be received.[144]

Toby advised Burnet on July 13 that "we have shipped on board the *Flora*: 500 cartridge boxes, bayonet scabbards and belts; and have ordered 500 caps."[145]

Again, on July 16, Toby mentioned the *Flora's* cargo, embarking that date: 500 cartridge boxes, bayonet belts and scabbards; and 10,000 musket and rifle flints "as per bill of lading included. We have under way 500 caps and 500 haversacks." On board also, he advised, were one hundred volunteers of the regiment of the Ladies Cavalry of Louisville. "We have shipped them with a few rifles, shirts, provisions, shoes, etc."[146]

July 20, Toby sent to Galveston aboard the brig *Good Hope* two cases containing: 12 doz. striped twilled pants; 2 doz. duck twilled pants; 2 doz. duck shirts; 24 doz. white cotton pants. On July 23, he added to the cargo: tin cups; canteens; and three cases containing cotton and duck shirts and pantaloons.[147]

On August 10, Quartermaster General Almanzon Huston forwarded to General Burleson " a small supply of items including shoes, percussion caps, but not the requested flints. "Them we have not," he advised, "also clothing, that article has not yet arrived but is expected soon."[148] Huston also authorized Colonel Coleman to buy 75 horses, 75 saddles, and 75 bridles.[149]

The same date the quartermaster advised Lieutenant Martin K. Snell that "there is a lot clothing expected soon."[150]

On the 11th of July, Toby sent to Burnet a bill of lading for: 996 pint tin cups; 596 soldiers canteens; and four boxes containing 500 leather caps.[151] On the next day, Toby sent an invoice for "sundries shipped" to Velasco aboard the ship *Colonel Fannin* which included the 500 pint tin cups; 596 soldiers canteens and the 500 leather caps.[152]

These leather caps are undoubtedly the 500 caps mentioned earlier as being "under way." But what did they look like? They may have been the 1833 leather forage cap popularly known as the "hog-killer." It was meant to be very practical, its main selling point that it, despite being leather, could be folded up. It also had an ear warmer reflex flap that tied up when not needed but could be lowered in cold weather. In stations in the Southern or Southwest states the soldiers often cut the flap off because it made the headband uncomfortably warm most of the year. Like the Chrysler Airflow automobile of the 1930s, it was a revolutionary design not without merit, but so ugly it was rejected by the rank and file. As often as not, they kept wearing outmoded models, such as the 1826 garrison cap if they were still available. The "hog-killer" was regulation from 1833 to 1839 for many units, especially dragoons. Thus, presumably would not be available as surplus – unless certain ones were sold as such because of the unpopularity of that particular model. But the leather caps could have been *japanned* caps. *Japanned* meant the top was waterproofed with a black enamel or lacquer which produced a durable glossy finish. These, usually of leather, were very popular then. Another possibility was sealskin, like the cap of the New Orleans Greys. This was also a popular cap of the times. It was virtually identical to a military soft top fatigue cap, except for the material of the band and crown. Stephen F. Austin is described as wearing "a *sealskin cap* with reflex edges turned down to protect his ears," by W.P. Zuber in *My 80 Years in Texas*.[153] These several variations were also known as *hunting* caps. Many were seen on the European emigrants coming to Texas, especially Germans.

Such caps were available in New Orleans, as evidenced by advertisements in newspapers there, such as this one turned up by the research of Ed Miller:

HATS & CAPS – the subscribers have received recent arrivals, 50 cases blk Beaver hats, 50 do Silk do, 100 imitation Beaver do, 100 do Roram do, 50 youths and childrens do, Also a complete assortment of Otter, Cloth and Seal caps, which are offered for sale on liberal terms, at No 10, Chartres St. by JAS. EVANS & Co.[154]

Shortly after San Jacinto, responding to the request of the Texas government, General Edmund P. Gaines, commander of the U.S. forces in Louisiana, sent several units from his command to Nacogdoches. Ostensibly there were to intimidate the Indians of the area from going on the warpath against either Texians or Americans along the border. Their presence was also to discourage a re-invasion by the Mexicans. Of these American soldiers, many now became true deserters, not the San Jacinto temporary type, and remained in Texas. An American officer sent in mid-summer of 1836 to get them back found about two hundred uniformed U.S. soldiers in the vicinity of Nacogdoches unwilling to return. Most joined the Texas Army, presumably still wearing their American uniforms.[155]

From New Matagorda Bay on August 12, First Lieutenant J. Combs wrote to a Dr. A.W. Haynes in Bardstown, Kentucky regarding the arrival of volunteers, "there are three vessels now in the bay that have just been unloaded of provisions and clothing."[156]

From his office at Quintana, Quartermaster Almanzon Huston wrote to his Assistant Quartermaster on August 13, "As it is important that there should be clothing furnished the army you will therefore return to Mr. Mann the *tailors* you took from him and provide other laborers for the mill. They cannot be but of little use to the mill as they are tradesman, *but they can be of great use in making clothes for the army*."[157]

Later that month, General Rusk sent a letter from army headquarters at Coleto to interim President Burnet containing needs of the army. In addition to a variety of flints, it requested: 2,000 cotton shirts, pantaloons, roundabouts, shoes, and caps … "without which the army can't be kept together (for many of the men are naked and will be more so in thirty days time)."[158] A bit of hyperbole there, perhaps, for if one is naked, how can one become *more* naked? It reminds one that the military mind hasn't changed much; for in our times during the Cold War exaggerated and alarming reports of Russian strength being superior to that of our own forces always seemed to emanate from the military just before Congress was to consider their share of the budget.

Burnet forwarded the list on August 30 to the Texian agency in New Orleans, Thomas Toby & Brother, adding "they are indispensable." The artillery also had wants, he advised, and "Captain Durocher of the artillery goes to your city in fact to procure them. I trust it will be in your power to supply his wants." Burnet included a supplemental list for: 120 suits for the (artillery) men; also blankets; 2 bugles; 4 drums; 4 fifes; 500 muskets for the infantry; 200 cartridge boxes; and *12 pounds of gray thread*.[159] This latter item must have been for repair or creation of uniforms, possibly by the tailors requested by the Quartermaster General A. Huston, very possibly using the gray cloth and lace trim ordered by Commissary General Forbes.

On September 1, Thomas Toby advised Burnet that he had shipped to the commanding officer at Matagorda Bay for use of the army: 70 canteens; 8 doz. tin cups; 400 pair brogans; 11_ doz. white wool hats; 20 doz. Russia duck shirts; 10 doz. brown linen pantaloons; 20 doz. blue twilled pantaloons; 17 doz. brown jackets; 303 best red flannel shirts – "and we shall ship by first vessel for Galveston" – 40 doz. duck shirts; 5 doz. brown linen pantaloons; 25 doz. blue drilling pantaloons; 297 red flannel shirts; 200 pair brogans.[160] Considering the dates, the load of supplies sent to Matagorda Bay may been those mentioned by Lieutenant Combs.

The wool hats need explanation: beaver hats were the best quality, wool the worst. Wool hats were cheap, had a low crown that was rounded and just covered the top of the head, with a brim that turned up because otherwise it had a tendency to lose its shape. In short, they were ugly. Even well into the twentieth century "wool hats" was a derisive nickname for Southern rednecks, the class who wore them. It would be hard to imagine them being well received by the Texas troops. But in the only photograph of Mier expedition men, taken while they were captives of the Mexicans, *three of the four in the picture are wearing wool hats*.

From his "executive office" (actually his home), Burnet wrote Toby on September 3 that Robert E. Handy was on his way to Philadelphia to sell Texas script; adding "the article of clothing for the army is one of considerable interest. Mr. Handy says he would see to the execution of any order on the subject either in New York or Philadelphia where the article could probably be had on better terms than anywhere else. While on the subject, I will remark that *the clothing should be uniform* and that winter clothing will now be wanted." He added, "PS – a uniform button is much wanted to distinguish our national dress. If you could make arrangements with a manufacturer through the aide of Mr. Handy or otherwise, it would be well to have some manufactured. Our distinguishing button is a star central, letters 'Texas' semi-circle above, letters, T.A. below, the button to be a little oval."[161] The desire for uniformity was overdue. For, while gray uniforms had been designated for field service, and blue was the *de facto* color for dress uniforms, the agents in the

United States, as can be seen, were until now sending anything in the way of clothing they could lay their hands on, whether military or not, and without regard to color. The only uniformity so far was the *cut* – usually roundabout jackets, pantaloons (usually white duck), brogans, and caps, which may have been of several styles. Throughout the military history of Texas caps seem to have been preferred over the broad-brimmed slouch hats so beloved by moviemakers.

Toby invoiced the government on September 25 for a shipment to Galveston aboard the schooner *Congress*: 10 cannon; 2 gun carriages; 4 cases russet brogans; 5 cases containing – 40 doz. duck shirts; 5 doz. brown linen pantaloons; 25 doz. blue drilling pantaloons; 297 red flannel shirts; 29 soldiers canteens; 17 pint cups.[162]

The last shipment from Toby to the provisional government went on board the *Colonel Fannin* September 29, consigned to Colonel James Morgan, military commander of Galveston: one bale Lowell cotton for shirts; 4 cases of shoes; 2 cases of clothing and canteens.[163] The cotton for shirts again demonstrates that the government was making at least a feeble effort to have a portion of its military clothing produced in Texas.

## Houston Runs for President

When departing to seek his destiny in Texas, Sam Houston had confided to his friend McIntosh, a deacon of the First Baptist Church of Nashville that he expected to "set in motion a little two-horse republic under the lone star," with the fond expectation he would be its first president,[164] according to Z.N. Morrell, an old Houston friend, who described himself as an "old Texan" and a "cane-break Baptist preacher"[165] in his book *Flowers and Fruits from the Wilderness or 36 Years in Texas and Seven Winters in Honduras*.

In addition to those who came to fight, many others now came to Texas as genuine emigrants. Soon the newcomers outnumbered the original Texians. All had absorbed the image of Sam Houston from reading newspaper accounts in the United States, which universally praised him as "the Sword of San Jacinto."[166] He was in their uncritical eyes *the savior of Texas*.

Charitably ignored by the adoring newcomers was Houston's sordid past among the Indians. He boasted that during the years he lived with the Cherokees they called him "The Raven." Originally they did, but as his tenure with them progressed they changed his nickname to "Big Drunk."[167] Passed over too was that in preparation for his new destiny to evolve in Texas he abandoned his Indian wife, Tiana Rogers and his mixed-blood children,* thus shedding the onerous stigma of "squaw man."

Traditionally a military victor outweighs a man of peace, particularly at election time. Stephen F. Austin, who had been the foremost to create and nurture the American settlements through fifteen difficult years, was bitter that Houston, whom his respectable colonists considered the leader of the rough and tumble latecomers, was now the hero of the day, Austin's accomplishments now largely ignored.

"A successful military chieftain is hailed with admiration and applause and monuments perpetuate his fame," he wrote to his cousin Mary Austin Holly, "but the bloodless pioneer of the wilderness, like the corn and cotton he causes to spring where it never grew before, attracts no notice. No slaughtered thousands or smoking cities attest to his devotion to the cause of human happiness, and he is regarded by the mass of the world as an humble instrument to pave the way for others."[168]

As required by the constitution drawn up in March by the General Assembly, interim President Burnet on July 23 called for an election to be held September 5 to elect a president, vice president, and other officials and to ratify the constitution.

There were two principal candidates: Sam Houston and Stephen F. Austin.

All of the newcomers were ardently for Houston, the "old timers" for Austin. Even some of Houston's most vocal critics during the campaign, seeing the inevitability of his getting the office, now suddenly became supporters. Nevertheless, some Houston partisans, wanting a sure thing for their candidate, spread malicious slanders about Austin "of the wildest character."[169] Austin did

no campaigning of his own, except to have published in the *Texas Telegraph*, whose editor Gail Borden** was one of the old timers, a long letter of rebuttal answering each and every charge. It did no good.

Sam Houston, whatever his deficiencies in morals or strategy, now the hero of the hour of America's *Manifest Destiny* expansionism, was elected president of the new Republic of Texas. Stephen F. Austin, whom even Houston was later to concede was "the father of Texas," received only 587 votes to Houston's 5,119.[170]

October 22, 1836, Sam Houston, "Old San Jacinto," took the oath of office as the first President of the Republic of Texas. Mirabeau B. Lamar, another hero of the revolution, was sworn in as Vice President.

What had been only a desperate dream was now a reality. Texas was now an independent nation.

Houston's aim was for annexation to the United States as soon as practical. He furloughed the army and cut funds for the navy to reduce expenses. In his view, only a militia was required until annexation was accomplished. Lamar, the second president, had a totally different objective. He opposed annexation. Instead, he envisioned Texas as becoming a mighty empire extending all the way to the Pacific coast, to rival the United States. For this he needed a strong military, smartly uniformed and equipped with the latest in weaponry. And he created it.

During the ten years of Texas independence, the army and navy of the new republic, backed up by a militia described by a British consul as "the most formidable militia, for their numbers, in the world,"[171] fought enemies within and without. There were triumphs and disasters. Finally, financially exhausted, Texas joined the United States in 1846, but even then under the special terms afforded to no other state.

From the Texas Revolution and the decade of the Republic of Texas, Texans still retain a unique mystique. As recently as 1997, a poll conducted by Frank Luntz for the public relations firm of Temerlin McClain revealed that nearly one-fourth of Texas residents considered themselves Texans first, Americans second. According to

---

*The famous folk comedian Will Rogers claimed descent from the union of Sam Houston and his Cherokee wife, Tiana Rogers.

**Gail Borden later switched from printing to the milk business, becoming famous for patenting the first successful milk condensing process in 1856. Borden condensed milk is still a popular product today.

Luntz, it demonstrates a stunningly high rate of identity with a state, probably unmatched in any of the other 49 states.[172]

This should be no surprise to anyone. The Texas Revolution in itself was an extraordinary addition to the saga of American expansionism; with its rugged, self-reliant and independent frontiersmen, in for the most part homemade uniforms or homespun, armed mostly with squirrel rifles, defeating the seasoned professionals of the pompous and unscrupulous Mexican dictator, Santa Anna.

This was an enemy with a reputation for cruelty, cunning, and cowardice. As one New Orleans newspaper described them, "the Mexicans have shown themselves incapable of observing the rules and practices of honorable war between civilized nations."[173] In the Texas Revolution were two of the most dramatic battles of all time, anywhere: *the Alamo* and *San Jacinto*. Each will forever remain a source of strength and pride for all future generations.

*Chapter Three*

# The Mexican Army in Texas

When notified that his brother-in-law, General Cos, was besieged at Bexar by the Texian rebels, the Mexican dictator Santa Anna organized the Army of Operations Against Texas to put down the revolt. It was assembled in northern Mexico in late 1835. Its initial composition was:

**Staff**

Commander-in-Chief, general of divisions, Antonio López de Santa Anna; Second in Command, general of divisions, Vicente Filisola; Major General, General of Brigade, Juan Arago; Quartermaster, Brevet General, Colonel Adrian Woll; Commanding General of Artillery, Lieutenant Colonel Tomas Requena.

**First Division**

*First Division of Infantry*, under Brigade General Joaquim Ramírez y Sesma, 1,350 men and 8 cannon; made up of Permanent Battalion, Matamoros, 272 men; Permanent Battalion, Jiminez, 274 active men; Active Battalion, San Luis Potosi, 425 men; *Cavalry*, Permanent Regiment, Dolores, 290 men; *Artillery*, 8 cannon of different calibers, 62 men.

**Second Division**

*Second Division of Infantry*, under Santa Anna himself, 2,827 men and 12 cannon. First Brigade, under Brevet General, Colonel Antonio Gaona, 1,577 men:

consisting of: *Infantry*, Permanent Battalion, Aldama, 393 men; Active Battalion, Toluca, 324 men; Active Battalion, Queretero, 375 men; Battalion, Guanajuato, 391 men; (part of) Active Battalion, San Luis Potosi, 31 men; *Artillery*, 6 cannon of different calibers, 63 men. Second Brigade, under Brevet General, Colonel Eugenio Tolsa, 1,250 men of the following units: *Infantry*, Permanent Battalion, Guerrero, 403 men; First Active Battalion, (state of) Mexico, 363 men; Active Battalion, Guadalajara, 428 men; *Artillery*, 6 cannon of various calibers, 60 men.

**Cavalry Brigade**

*Cavalry Brigade*, under Brigade General Juan José Andrade, 680 men of the following units: Permanent Regiment, Tampico, 250 men; Permanent Regiment, Cuautla, 180 men; Auxiliary Companies, Guanajuato, 180 men; Auxiliary Companies (partial) San Luis Potosi, 40 men; Auxiliary Companies (partial), Bajio, 30 men.

**Engineers**

*Sapper Battalion*, commanded by Lieutenant Colonel Augustin Amat.

Thus the Army of Operations Against Texas initially consisted of 5,050 troops and 20 artillery pieces. They expected to add to their number those under Cos, who had about 500 men, and some Presidials (local militia). So the total was to be more than 5,500, plus the 20 cannons, by the end of 1835.

On learning that Cos had surrendered San Antonio and retreated to Laredo, Santa Anna changed his plans. Instead of proceeding to Laredo and advancing from there to San Antonio, he would take a circuitous route via Presidio de Rio Grande and surprise the Texians by arriving from the northwest. Santa Anna revised his organization somewhat as they departed for Texas. The First Division was renamed the Vanguard Brigade, and the Second Division was to be broken up into brigades. These brigades were now to be as follows:

*First Infantry Brigade*, under Brevet General, Colonel Antonio Gaona, Permanent Battalion, Aldama under Lieutenant Colonel Gregorio Urunulea; First Active Battalion, Toluca, under General Francisco Duque; Active Battalion, Queretaro, Colonel Cayetano Montoya; Active Battalion, Guanajuato, Brevet General, Lieutenant Colonel Ignacio Pretalia; Sapper Battalion, Lieutenant Colonel Augustin Amat, some infantry Presidials, plus 6 artillery pieces and crews.

*Second Infantry Brigade*, under Brevet General, Colonel Eugenio Tolsa; Permanent Battalion, Morelos, under Colonel Nicolás Condelle, Permanent Battalion, Guerrero, Colonel Manuel de Cespedes; First Active Battalion, (state of) Mexico, Brevet Colonel, Lieutenant Colonel Francisco Quintero; Active Battalion, Guadalajara, Colonel José Manuel Canedo; (part of the) Active Battalion, Tres Villas, Brevet Colonel, Lieutenant Colonel Augustin Alcerreca, and six pieces of artillery and their crews.

Plus more troops were to advance from Matamoros under General José Urrea. Though more reinforcements were expected, Santa Anna ordered an advance in mid January. His army now was made up of: 4,473 infantry, 1,024 cavalry, 182 gunners, 185 sappers, 60 foot and 95 mounted presidials: *a grand total of over 6,000*. Most were seasoned regulars, others hastily recruited for this campaign.

In early 1836, General Nicolas Bravo reported the equipment for his field forces in Texas included: English fusils with bayonets, ramrods, and locks; rifle cartridges with powder and lead ball of 19 ardames (1 3/16 oz.); rifle flints; 12 caliber infantry cartridges of cloth nap; for the mounted artillery company sabers with steel scabbards; English terceroles (carbines), rifle cartridges with one ounce lead balls, carbines, and quick-matches.[1] Other equipment included 1822 model fusils, and British Tower smoothbore muzzleloader flintlock muskets (the "Brown Bess") caliber .753 lead ball, sold by the British to Mexico as unserviceable surplus. These had a range of less than 100 yards,[2] and had a terrible kick. To avoid this, the Mexican soldiers often held their weapon below the shoulder when firing which prevented them from taking accurate aim. British-made Baker carbines were also issued to some units. They were rifled,[3] thus superior to the Brown Bess. While use of the by now obsolete Brown Bess by the Mexican Army has often been criticized, this was the weapon that conquered India.

There were also some English Cosgrove rockets, which may have seen some limited use at the Alamo.[4]

Mexican uniforms have always been a bewildering variety of gaudy and colorful designs, differing often by regiments and even battalions. Officers were especially magnificently attired. All Mexican uniform patterns were hand-me-downs from Spanish colonial days. And these were heavily influenced by Napoleonic fashions, as Santa Anna was a great admirer of Napoleon and self-described as "The Napoleon of the West." During the Texas campaign full dress was usually worn, even during the distasteful episode of executing the Goliad prisoners.

Following is a sampling of the Mexican uniforms worn by the Army of Operations Against Texas.

★　　★　　★

*Plate 13 (page 65)*

# SANTA ANNA

General Antonio de Santa Anna Pérez de Lebrón dominated Mexican politics for many decades and was president of Mexico when the Texas Revolution began in 1835.

Enraged, Santa Anna personally led his Army of Operations Against Texas, vowing to exterminate the rebels and any foreigners who aided them. A strutting peacock, he was a man of many eye-boggling uniforms. Here he is in the one artist-historian Joseph Hefter depicted him as having worn during the siege of the Alamo.[5] Probably he had several different uniforms along on the Texas campaign. There is also a photograph of one with even more gold braid on the chest, which was said to have been captured with his abandoned baggage at San Jacinto. For many years it was loaned to any San Jacinto veteran to wear at his wedding. It finally disappeared, presumably not being returned after one such loan.[6]

Santa Anna's first excursion into Texas was as a Spanish officer assisting in the quelling of the Gutiérrez-Magee filibustering expedition in 1813. At the battle of the Medina he was cited for bravery.

Behind the dictator is the oft-described blood red flag meaning *no quarter*, a hand-me-down from the Spanish battles with the Moors, who were said to have first used it. Exactly what it looked like is questionable. Some have shown it as a solid red. However Henry Arthur McArdle, the artist who did the historical paintings *Dawn at the Alamo* and *The Battle of San Jacinto*, shows it in his Alamo painting as having the white skull and crossbones on it. He shows it carried by the Mexicans as they entered the Alamo compound. When Santa Anna first arrived in San Antonio he had it flow atop the San Fernando church on the main plaza.[7]

McArdle conducted exhaustive correspondence with several Texas veterans and Santa Anna himself in an effort to insure the authenticity of his works.

Some histories show the dictator's name as *Santa Ana*, however in the correspondence from the Mexican leader, his signature clearly reads *Santa Anna*.

★  ★  ★

*Plate 14 (page 66)*
## BATTALÓN MATAMORAS

This is the uniform worn at the battles of the Alamo and San Jacinto by the Permanent Battalion of Matamoros.[8]

Behind is the battalion flag which was captured at San Jacinto and now reposes in the Texas State Archives.

In the background is the Alamo compound as it must have originally looked, including a bell tower, when first completed. In at least one publication this view is mislabeled as taken from an oil painting done by Mexican army Colonel Juan José Sánchez-Navarro in 1836, presumably during the siege. Aside from the improbability of the officer having enough leisure during the thirteen-day siege to complete an oil painting, during the siege, the bell tower no longer existed; the chapel roof was as shown in plate 4 (Travis).

★  ★  ★

*Plate 15 (page 67)*
## SAPPER

Sappers were an engineering and work unit, with the name sapper coming from the laying of saps (mines) in tunnels dug under enemy fortifications. Like the other Mexican units in Texas, the sappers seem to have worked in their full dress, though sometimes doffing their shakos for the tasseled fatigue cap shown. While working they often wore the gloves, leather apron, and spats.[9]

The flag behind the sapper is from a sketch attributed to Sánchez-Navarro (this one more likely to be authentic) made at the Alamo with this banner supposedly flying atop the chapel. It has been presumed the two stars represent Coahuila and Texas when they were combined as one state.[10] Traditionally sappers wore beards.

★  ★  ★

*Plate 16 (page 68)*
## LANCER

The lancers and cavalry with the Army of Operations Against Texas had several varieties of uniforms, from the uniform contracts of 1832 and 1833. Shown here is the 1832 model. There was little difference between the two contracts. Both styles were worn until at least 1837, possibly beyond.[11]

The lancer shown here wears a leather jockey cap with a vertical tricolor plume on the left side in the Mexican national colors and a black plume in the center of either goat or horse hair. Trousers were dark blue, sometimes gray. They were cloth with leather reinforcement on the seat and down the insides of the legs. Weaponry was a nine-foot lance, a sword, carbine, and two saddle pistols.[12]

Dragoons were similarly uniformed and equipped, according to Alamo expert Rueben Marmaduke Potter in his correspondence with the historical artist McArdle.[13]

The horse equipment is well illustrated in a rare paperback, perhaps now out of print since the death of Hefter, *El Soldado Mexicano, 1837-1847* by Nieto, Brown Hefter, (in both Spanish and English). Despite the dates in the title it also has information on uniforms and equipment before 1837.

★　★　★

*Plate 17 (page 69)*
## LIEUTENANT COLONEL JOSÉ NICOLÁS DE LA PORTILLA

Lieutenant Colonel José Nicolás de la Portilla was with the Active Battalion of Tres Villas, and was the officer who carried out Santa Anna's infamous order to execute the Texian prisoners captured at Goliad (Coleto).

There is a photograph of Portilla in this dark blue uniform, with his for-and-aft chapeau with its tricolor rosette,[14] though it was undoubtedly taken after the Texas campaign. Nevertheless it was probably what he wore in Texas as the regulation uniforms of 1832 and 1833 were worn at least until 1837 and perhaps beyond.

Fannin surrendered his command, more than 400 men, to General José Urrea unconditionally, but with the verbal understanding that they would receive clemency and be repatriated to the United States. However, when Urrea conveyed this to Santa Anna, the dictator angrily reminded him of orders issued at the beginning of the campaign that all colonists and foreigners found with guns in their hands were to be considered pirates and executed. Urrea, though unhappy with this rebuke, nevertheless when he departed Goliad left in the hands of Portilla the repugnant task of executing the prisoners.

On Palm Sunday, March 27, Portilla had the prisoners awakened and marched eastward out of Fort Defiance. They were lulled into a feeling of optimism by assurances they were to be marched to the coast and returned to the United States. Part way out, they were halted and without warning gunned down by their guards. Only about thirty escaped. Fannin and other wounded unable to march were executed in the presidio. Dr. Jack Shackleford, the commander of the Red Rovers and a few other Texians who were medical personnel were spared to care for the Mexican wounded.

Behind Portilla is the flag of the Tres Villas Battalion.[15]

★　★　★

*Plate 18 (page 70)*
## ACTIVO BATALLÓN DE TRES VILLAS

The Activo Batallón de Tres Villas was a volunteer militia unit drawn from the three villages of Jalapa, Córdoba, and Orizaba in the tropical region. Many of the members were Indians, Blacks or *Chinos* (Indian and Black mixed-bloods).

In February of 1836 the Tres Villas were attached to the division commanded by General Urrea marching on Goliad. They had several colonels but by Goliad their commanding officer was Lieutenant colonel José Nicolás de la Portilla (plate 17). The Tres Villas took part in Urrea's pursuit of Fannin's retreating command and the battle of Coleto. Following their surrender, Fannin and his men were imprisoned in the compound of the Mission La Bahia del Espiritu Santu de Zuniga (which Fannin renamed Fort Defiance). There they were guarded by the Tres Villas and others in Urrea's division. The Tres Villas were among those who carried out the atrocious massacre of the Texian prisoners. According to Lieutenant Colonel José de las Pena, "they were greatly moved upon being required to duty so alien to their rules, so degrading to brave soldiers."[16]

Because of some confusion from misconduct and desertions of several officers supposedly in command, the Tres Villas never reached San Jacinto.

They had both dress and fatigue uniforms for the Texas campaign but, because they came from the tropical region, no overcoats, thus suffered more than the other units from the cold.

Depicted here is a corporal in the 1833 contract full dress. The yellow stripe on his left arm denotes his rank. He is holding the India pattern Brown Bess musket, pattern 1797. The Mexican version was post-1809, with the Mexican eagle stamped on the lock plate, and it had a reinforced cock throat. His shako was eight inches tall and almost cylindrical, topped by a small, elongated pom pom. His dark blue coat is of Queretero cloth with a lining of "coarse cloth." Collars, epaulets, and cuffs were red, with the unit initials on the collar. He was issued one dress pair of trousers of medium or dark blue and two pair of white sailcloth; two white linen shirts; two black velveteen stocks; two pair of black shoes; and one barracks cap with tassel (similar to the one depicted in the Sapper, plate 15). He carried a short sword in addition to a bayonet.[17]

In the background is the Mission La Bahia del Espiritu Santu complex. This complex, considerably damaged and deteriorated over the years has now been fully restored by private funds from the Kathryn Stoner O'Connor Foundation. It is a tourist attraction well worth visiting. The name has now been shortened to Presidio La Bahia.

★ ★ ★

*Plate 19 (page 71)*

## MEXICAN INFANTRY WHITE UNIFORM

Some have questioned whether white uniforms were along on the Texas expedition, considering the severity of the Texas weather in the early months of the year. But they were among the Mexican uniforms, according to Rueben Marmaduke Potter, who furnished information to the artist McArdle for his paintings of the battles of the Alamo and San Jacinto. In his letters to the artist, Potter described the white uniform as "a fatigue suit, consisting of white cotton round jackets and trousers, with black shoulder straps crossed on the breast. Head dress was the old-fashioned black shako of leather or felt. (illegible) the usual pom pom and metallic trimmings such as a letter or number. It often had drawn on it, a close fitting white cloth cover with the decorations outside, worsted shoulder knots of red, blue or green worn by some battalions."[18] While Potter was considered an expert on the Alamo because of his writings on the subject, during the revolution he was representing an American commercial house in Matamoros, thus was not an actual witness to the military action, though he may have seen the Mexican troops while some were in Matamoros.

On the Texas campaign the crossbelts were white. Jacket collar and cuffs were red as were the shoulder wings. Shako ornaments were sometimes removed when the white cover was worn. The white uniform, with the cap pom pom removed and the brass plate covered is shown in one of the contemporary sketches of Mexican costumes by Linati. While shoes were supposedly standard issue, in his detailed orders for the assault on the Alamo, Santa Anna instructed, "The troops will wear shoes or *sandals*."[19]

The soldier holds an 1809 modification of the Brown Bess musket, the model used by the Mexicans. For many decades it was the standard weapon of the British Army. This is the arm that served them in the American Revolution, the War of 1812, against Napoleon, and was also used by the East India Company in India. The Mexicans used the Brown Bess even through the Mexican War of 1846-1848.

The brass hat ornament in the background is one of several variations worn by the Mexican infantry.[20]

★ ★ ★

*Plate 20 (page 72)*

## PRESIDIAL TROOPER

Presidials (*presidiales*) were local militia mainly for defense against Indians. They were usually armed with escopetes, a short, but not particularly accurate or effective, smoothbore carbine. Despite its drawbacks, the escopete was widely used throughout the southwest from the late seventeenth century to the 1840s. They were often equipped with lances, also, and while an unusual weapon in the eyes of Americans, a lasso. The lasso was, surprisingly, a very effective tool. As the steamboat *Yellow Stone* moved downriver on the Brazos a Mexican audaciously attempted to lasso one of its twin stacks.

Uniforms of the presidials varied greatly by locality across the Southwest. For what they looked like in Texas we had a watercolor by Lino Sánchez y Tapia, commissioned by Jean-Louis Berlandier, the botanist of the Mier y Terán commission that toured Texas in the late 1820s. This watercolor was done from sketches made on the expedition by Berlandier and José María Sánchez y Tapia, the originals of which are now lost.

The presidial shown here is taken from the Sánchez watercolor. In another Sánchez painting of the inhabitants of Texas a ranchero is wearing an identical top hat and his horse equipments is virtually identical. The peculiar but practical leather flaps on the front of the saddle are called *armas*. They were, and still are, used in lieu of chaps.[21]

Behind the presidial is a lance pennant sometimes used instead of the plain red one. The message, *NO DAMOS CUARTEL* (we don't give quarter), reiterates the heartless message of the *deguello*, the bugle call that carries the same cruel warning. The white skull and crossbones reinforce the opinion of the artist McArdle that the blood red flag carried by Santa Anna had this symbol, rather than being plain as some historians had suggested.[22]

The presidials attached to the Army of Operations Against Texas were sixty afoot and ninety-five mounted; a total of only 155. They were colorful but not particularly effective.

★　★　★

*Plate 21 (page 73)*
## COLONEL JUAN MORALES

Colonel Juan Morales participated in the battles of the Alamo and San Jacinto.

At the Alamo Santa Anna divided his attack force into four columns, with Morales commanding the fourth. Morales' column attacked the southwest corner, and it was the first to breach the wall and fight its way into the compound.

At San Jacinto Morales was temporarily in command of the Permanent Battalion of Guerrero. Both he and the unit flag, pictured behind him, were captured.

The coat he is wearing was appropriated by one of the Texian guards. It is now on display at the San Jacinto Monument, one of the few, albeit incomplete, uniforms extant from the Texas Revolution.

The battalion flag is in storage at the Texas Archives, along with other captured Mexican flags, not available for the public to view.

Behind Morales is the only Mexican cannon at San Jacinto, the Golden Standard, a formidable 12-pounder. Fortunately for the Texians, its gunners fled after getting off only three shots. It later became a part of the artillery of the Republic of Texas. A replica is displayed at the Texas Military Forces Museum at Camp Mabry, headquarters of the Texas National Guard, Austin, Texas.

# *Epilogue*

The Texas Revolution was summed up succinctly by former United States President Theodore Roosevelt:

> Any one who has ever been on the frontier, and who knows anything whatever of the domineering, masterful spirit and bitter race prejudices of the white frontiersmen, will acknowledge at once that it was out of the question that the Texans should long continue under Mexican rule; and it would have been a great misfortune if they had. It was out of the question to expect them to submit to the mastery of the weaker race, which they were supplanting. Whatever might be the pretexts alleged for revolt, the real reasons were to be found in the deeply marked differences of race, and in the absolute unfitness of the Mexicans then to govern themselves, to say nothing of governing others.[1]

Race was by no means the entire explanation, however. Equally important was the total difference in political idealogies. Mexico writhed in chronic political corruption and despotism, whereas the Texians in their previous country were accustomed to considerable constitutionally guaranteed liberty. The realities of Mexican misrule gradually soured them on any hope for change, especially after the constitution of 1824 was discarded. The liberal element among Tejanos joined with them in revolt and, while a minority, also fought against the tyranny of the central government. The Anglo population in Texas at the time of the revolution was approximately 25,000; the Mexicans less than 5,000. Thus in the fight for democracy versus dictatorship, the ratio of Anglos to Mexicans in the revolutionary army was roughly equivalent to their percentages of the Texas population.

*Plates*

First Company of TEXAN VOLUNTEERS. GOD & LIBERTY FROM NEW-ORLEANS

©Bruce Marshall
KCWE

New Orleans Greys
Texas Revolution

Alabama Red Rovers
*service uniform*
Texas Revolution

*Alabama Red Rovers*
*dress uniform*
*Texas Revolution*

*Lt. Col. William B. Travis*
commander of the Alamo

*Texas Revolution*

Col. Sidney Sherman
Kentucky volunteers
Texas Revolution
the Newport Rifles

Col. John A. Wharton
Adjutant General/Texas Army
Texas Revolution

Captain Charles Hawkins
Texas Navy
Texas Revolution

### the Common Soldier
#### Texas Army
### Texas Revolution

American Army volunteers
Texas Revolution

Edward Burleson
Texas Army
the "Come and take it" flag
and the Gonzales cannon
Texas Revolution

Moses Austin Bryan
fought at San Jacinto
the "twin sisters" in background

Texas Revolution

OUR
COUNTRY'S
GHTS
OR
EATH

*Gen. Thomas Jefferson Chambers*
*Texas Army*

*Texas Revolution*

*Gen. Antonio Lopez de Santa Anna*
*Mexican dictator*

*Texas Revolution*

*Batallón Matamoros*
*Mexican Army*
*Texas Revolution*

Sapper
Mexican Army
Texas Revolution

Lancer
Mexican Army
Texas Revolution

Lt. Col. José Nicolás de la Portilla
Goliad Commandant
Mexican Army

Texas Revolution

Activo Batallón de Tres Villas
Mexican Army
Texas Revolution

*Mexican Infantry*
white uniform
*Texas Revolution*

*Presidial Trooper*
*Mexican Army auxiliary*
*The Texas Revolution*

*Colonel Juan Morales*
*Mexican Army*
*(captured at San Jacinto)*
*Texas Revolution*

# Notes

**INTRODUCTION**

1. Jenkins, ed., *Amasa Turner's Account*, 1.
2. Hardin, *Texian Iliad*, 289.
3. Webb, ed., *Handbook of Texas*, vol. II, 554.

**BACKGROUND**

1. Jackson, *Los Tejanos*, 15.
2. Barker, *Mexico and Texas*, 53.
3. Webb, ed., *Handbook of Texas*, vol. II, 554.
4. Wortham, *History of Texas*, vol. I, 13.
5. Oates, *Republic of Texas*, 13.
6. Dewees, *Letters*, 71.
7. Hunter, comp., *Life of Creed Taylor*, 8.
8. Smithwick, *Evolution of a State*, 45.
9. Barker, *Mexico and Texas*, 1821-1835, 52-53; Barker, *Life of Stephen F. Austin*, 261.
10. Ibid., 53.
11. Smithwick, *Evolution of a State*, 106.
12. Morton, *Terán and Texas*, 104-105; Barker, *Life of Stephen F. Austin*, 412-413.
13. Ibid., 61.
14. Alamán letter to Mier y Terán of March 2, 1830 (transcript), UT-Austin.
15. Barker, *Life of Stephen F. Austin*, 412-413.
16. Yoakum, *History of Texas*, 274-275.

**TEXAS REVOLUTION AND ITS UNIFORMS**

1. Barker, *Life of Stephen F. Austin*, 412-413.
2. Jenkins, "Regulations for the National Militia of Coahuila and Texas," *Military History of Texas and the West*, Vol. 7, No. 3, 212; Hefter, *Army of the Republic of Texas*, Plate I; Ibid, *Uniforms of the Militia of Coahuila y Texas*, (n.d.).
3. *Texas Citizen Soldiers*, bulletin, star of the Republic Museum, (n.d.).
4. Jones, *The First Texas Rangers*, CMH Plate 457.
5. Hopewell, *Sam Houston*, 210.
6. Smithwick, *Evolution of a State*, 118; Wortham, *History of Texas*, vol. II, 366-420.

7. Ibid., 109-110.
8. Heath, Ebenezer S. Letter to his mother from Fort Defiance, Goliad, March 10, 1836. Davenport Collection, Center For American History, UT-Austin.
9. Ehrenberg, *Fahren und Schicksale Eines Deutschen in Texas*, 11-12 of transcript in Daughters of the Republic of Texas Library, San Antonio, from original in Eugene C. Barker Texas History Center, UT-Austin.
10. Cooke, Letter to his brother, Houston, August 7, 1839, Center for American History, UT-Austin.
11. This flag is displayed behind the speakers podium in the chamber of the House of Representatives in the Texas State Capitol.
12. Coleman, *Houston Displayed*, 4-5.
13. Ibid., *Houston Displayed*, 6-7.
14. Ibid., 8; Jenkins, ed., *Papers*, vol. II, 243.
15. Jackson, *Texas by Terán*, 81.
16. Jenkins, *Papers*, vol. II, 243.
17. Coleman, *Houston Displayed*, 14.
18. Jenkins, *Papers*, vol VIV, 243.
19. Wortham, *History of Texas*, vol. II, 414-418.
20. Ibid., vol. III, 14, concerning a desire to attack San Antonio, "…not more than one hundred men of the whole army (excepting the company of New Orleans Greys, who were willing and anxious for it, to a man) could be found willing to make the attack."
21. Ibid., vol. III, 72-76.
22. Ibid., 77.
23. Ibid., 89-90.
24. Ibid., 90.
25. Jenkins, *Papers*, vol. IV, 167.
26. Ibid., 297.
27. Ibid.,
28. Wortham, *History of Texas*, vol. III, 91.
29. Ibid., 103.
30. Jenkins, William H., "The Red Rovers of Alabama," *The Alabama Review*, (undated clip); Jones, Tom. *Alabama Red Rovers, 1835*, CMH Plate 502, (n.d.); Ehrenberg, *With Milam and Fannin*, 108.
31. Jenkins, John, ed., *Papers*, vol. IV, 512-513.
32. Ibid., 485.

33. Ibid, 499-500.

34. Gray, *Diary*, 125.

35. Wortham, *History of Texas*, vol. III, 180.

36. Ibid, 183.

37. Sánchez Lamego, *Siege*, 22.

38. Tinkle, *Thirteen Days*, 38.

39. Elting, Letter of March 25, 1995 to Bruce Marshall in author's possession.

40. Jenkins, ed., *Papers*, IV, 109.

41. Ibid., *Papers*, vol. VIV, Journal of the Convention at Washington on the Brazos, Texas, March 1-17, 1836, 287-344.

42. Potter, letter to H.A. McArdle, McArdle papers, Center for American History, UT-Austin.

43. Jenkins, ed., *Papers*, vol XIV, 287-344.

44. Wortham, *History of Texas*, vol. III, 184; Webb, ed., *Handbook of Texas*, vol. II, 795.

45. Copy of Travis' Letter of February 24, 1836 in author's possession. Original in Texas State Archives.

46. Webb, ed., *Handbook of Texas*, 502.

47. Sánchez Lamego, *Siege*, 35.

48. Gray, *Diary*, 137.

49. Sánchez Lamego, *Siege*, 34-36.

50. Santa Anna letter to Harry Arthur McArdle in McArdle notebook and letter file, Texas State Archives. In order to make his paintings of the battles of the Alamo and San Jacinto, McArdle corresponded with the Mexican dictator and several Texians who took part in the revolution. Santa Anna's assurance that all the Alamo defenders had died fighting may have been sincere; or to cover himself from claims published by some of his own followers that he had several captured or surrendered Texians executed.

51. Gaddy, ed., *Texas in Revolt*, 58.

52. Lord, *A Time to Stand*, 205; Jones and Elting, *The Alamo Garrison*, CMH Plate 385, (n.d.).

53. Sánchez Lamego, *Siege*, 26, 45.

54. Cox, *Romantic Flags*, 206.

55. Sánchez Lamego, *Siege*, 37.

56. *Austin American Statesman*, news article about Alamo flag, December 19, 1994.

57. Elting, Letter to Bruce Marshall of March 25, 1995 in author's possession.

58. Teja, *A Revolution Remembered*, 193; Rosenfield and Patton, *Texas History Movies*, 174.

59. Jenkins, *Papers*, vol. VIV, 343-344; Gammel, *Laws of Texas 1822-1897*; Jenkins, ed., *Papers*, vol. I, 93.

60. Ibid., vol. VIV, 343-344.

61. Hardin, *Texian Iliad*, 63.

62. Hunter, John W. Literary effort, Texas State Archives. unpublished manuscript, *Life of Creed Taylor, or Eighty-Three years on the Frontier of Texas*, 2-23/993. 32.

63. Coleman, *Houston Displayed*, 16.

64. Hunter, John W. Literary effort, 32.

65. *Southwestern Historical Quarterly*, LXXXIII, No. 4, April 1980. Explanatory note inside front cover.

66. Bate, *General Sidney Sherman*, 17.

67. Ibid., quote from *Cincinnati Daily Whig* of December 29, 1835, 17.

68. Ibid., *Daily Evening News* (city unspecified) of December 31, 1835, 17.

69. Delgado, *Mexican Account of San Jacinto*, 42.

70. Brown, *History of Texas*, vol. II, 4.

71. Ehrenberg, *With Milam and Fannin*, 136.

72. Brown, *History of Texas*, vol. I, 619-620.

73. Ibid.

74. Cox, *Romantic Flags*, 210.

75. Courtney, *After the Alamo*, 78; Coleman, *Houston Displayed*, 27.

76. Coleman, *Houston Displayed*, 27.

77. Yoakum, *History of Texas*, 305. Nevin, *The Texans*, 52.

78. Courtney, *After the Alamo*, 58; Wortham, *History of Texas*, 284.

79. Coleman, *Houston Displayed*, 22.

80. Hardin, *Texian Iliad*, 189.

81. Coleman, *Houston Displayed*, 28.

82. Tolbert, *Day of San Jacinto*, 86.

83. Letter from Rosenberg Library of February 1, 1995 to Bruce Marshall in author's possession; Army Papers, Texas State Archives, file 1218-1230.

84. Jenkins, ed., *Amasa Turner's Account*, 68.

85. Hardin, *Texian Iliad*, 247.

86. Amasa Turner, Letter to Jesse Billingsley of October 4, 1879, Billingsley papers, UT-Austin.

87. Coleman, *Houston Displayed*, 28.

88. Courtney, *After the Alamo*, 62; also Labadie, "The Battle of San Jacinto: an Eyewitness Account," in Oates, ed., *The Republic of Texas*, 32.

89. Jenkins, ed., *Amasa Turner's Account*, 72.

90. Ibid., 30-31. Courtney, *After the Alamo*, 63.

91. Labadie, "The Battle of San Jacinto: an Eyewitness Account," in Oates, ed., *Republic of Texas*, 31.

92. Hardin, *Texian Iliad*, 203-204.

93. Ibid.

94. James, *The Raven*, 249; Oates, ed., *The Republic of Texas*, 32.

95. Hardin, *Texian Iliad*, 206.

96. Wortham, *History of Texas*, vol. III, 279.

97. Tolbert, *Day of San Jacinto*, 86; Hardin, *Texian Iliad*, 283.

98. Steffen, *Horse Soldier*, vol. I, 96. Quoting military illustrator Charles McBarron, "Full dress had its uses on the frontier in impressing visiting Indians, and it was often worn."

99. Hefter, *Early Texas Uniforms, U.S. Infantry on Texas Border 1835 First Sergeant, fatigue dress*, one of series of color paintings in collections of Center for American History, UT-Austin; Kredel, *Uniforms of the American Army*, 7th (U.S.) Infantry 1835.

100. Jesse Billingsley letter to Amasa Turner of September 28, 1859 in Jesse Billingsley papers, Center for American History, UT-Austin.

101. Jenkins, ed., *Amasa Turner's Account*, 8; Coleman, *Houston Displayed*, 41, 73.

102. Jenkins, ed., *Amasa Turner's Account*, 8.

103. Oates, ed., *Republic of Texas*, 32.

104. Oates, *Republic of Texas*, 32; Hardin, *Texian Iliad*, 206.

105. Amasa Turner transcript, Center for American History, UT-Austin, 9.

106. Nevin, *The Texans*, 132; Hardin, *Texian Iliad*, 207; Oates, ed., *Republic of Texas*, quoting Labadie, 32.

107. Hardin, *Texian Iliad*, 207; Nevin, *The Texans*, 132; Haley, *Texas*, 80.

108. Oates, ed., *Republic of Texas*, 32; Jenkins, *Amasa Turner's Account*, 9; Coleman, *Houston Displayed*, 42.

109. *Galveston News*, June 23, 1855.

110. Wortham, *History of Texas*, vol. III, 296, 298; Delgado, *Mexican Account of San Jacinto*, 35.

111. Nevin, *The Texans*, 136.

112. Ibid.; Oates, ed., *Republic of Texas*, 32.

113. Nevin, *The Texans*, 136; Yoakum, *History of Texas*, 305-306, 300 (footnote).

114. Jenkins, ed., *Amasa Turner's Account*, 15.

115. Nevin, *The Texans*, 136.

116. Wortham, *History of Texas*, vol. III, 298; Delgado, *Mexican Account of San Jacinto*, 36.

117. Ibid., 298-299.

118. Jenkins, *Amasa Turner's Account*, 78; Turner transcript 16, Center for American History, UT-Austin.

119. Billingsley, Billingsley file, Center for American History, UT-Austin.

120. Nevin, *The Texans*, 137.

121. Hardin, *Texian Iliad*, 214.

122. Courtney, *After the Alamo*, 85-86; Oates, ed., *The Republic of Texas*, 33; Coleman, *Houston Displayed*, 44-45; Hardin, *Texian Iliad*, 214.

123. Billingsley, Billingsley papers, Center for American History, UT-Austin.

124. Jenkins, ed., *Amasa Turner's Account*, 14.

125. Hardin, *Texian Iliad*, quoting Turner, 216.

126. Nevin, *The Texans*, quoting Labadie, 33.

127. Jenkins, ed., *Amasa Turner's Account*, 15.

128. A. S. Burleson to Samuel Asbury, December 6, 1922, Samuel Asbury papers; and Emma Kyle Burleson papers, Texas State Archives.

129. Haley, *Texas*, 130.

130. Peña, *With Santa Anna in Texas*, 177-178.

131. Potter, "Escape of Karnes and Teal from Matamoros," letter to H.A. McArdle, *The Quarterly of the Texas State Historical Association*, vol. IV, No. 2, 71-81. October, 1900.

132. Ibid.

133. Ibid.

134. Webb, ed., Handbook of Texas, vol. II, 718.

135. Potter, "Escape of Karnes and Teal from Matamoros," letter to H.A. McArdle, *The Quarterly of the Texas State Historical Association*, vol. IV, No. 2, 71-81. October, 1900.

136. Matthews, *Ten Battle Flags*, Plate 9 by Bruce Marshall.

137. Gray, *Diary*, 178.

138. Ibid.

139. Army Papers, Texas State Archives, Box 1218-1228.

140. Jenkins, ed., *Papers*, vol. VI, 288.

141. Ibid., vol. VI, 299.

142. Ibid, vol. VII, 101.

143. Ibid., 143-144.

144. Ibid., 390-391.

145. Ibid., 467.

146. Ibid., 407.

147. Ibid., 507.

148. Ibid., vol. VIII, 23-24.

149. Ibid., 193.

150. Ibid., 195.

151. Ibid., 207.

152. Ibid., 216-217.

153. Zuber, *My Eighty Years in Texas*, 31.

154. *New Orleans Bee*, vol. IX, No. 50, November 21, 1835.

155. Nance, *After San Jacinto*, 16-17.

156. Jenkins, ed., *Papers*, vol. VII, 208.

157. Ibid., 227.

158. Ibid., 332-337.

159. Ibid., 350.

160. Ibid., 363.

161. Ibid., 457-458.

162. Ibid., vol. VIV, 7.

163. Ibid., 28.

164. Morrell, *Flowers and Fruits*, 20.

165. Ibid., in title and on 32; Webb, ed., *Handbook of Texas*, vol. II, 236.

166. Hardin, *Texian Iliad*, 289.

167. Haley, *Texas*, 41.

168. Ibid., 85.

169. Wortham, *History of Texas*, 362.

170. Ibid., 363.

171. *Texan Citizen Soldiers*, bulletin by Star of the Republic Museum, (n.d.).

172. "Poll shows Texans' allegiance to state," article in *Austin American Statesman*, 7-24-97.

173. Yoakum, *History of Texas*, Vol. I, 331, quoting from *The New Orleans Bulletin* of January 3, 1842.

## THE MEXICAN ARMY

1. Nieto, Brown, Hefter, *El Soldado Mexicano*, 53.

2. Ibid.

3. Ibid.

4. Huffines, *Blood and Noble Men*, 94-95.

5. Gaddy, *Texas in Revolt*, 60.

6. Haley, *Texas*, 83.

7. McArdle notebook and papers, Texas State Archives.

8. Gaddy, *Texas in Revolt*, frontpiece.

9. Huffines, *Blood and Noble Men*, 81-83.

10. Sánchez Lamego, *Siege*, 5, 26.

11. Nieto, Brown, Hefter, *El Soldado Mexicano*, illustration II.

12. Ibid., illustration I and III; *Cronica del Traje Militia en Mexico*, cover and 62; Hoffines, *Blood and Noble Men*, 81-83.

13. R.M. Potter letter to H.A. McArdle, McArdle notebook and papers, Texas State Archives.

14. Haley, *Texas*, 67.

15. Green, *Activo Batallón de Tres Villas*, 58.

16. Ibid., 55.

17. Ibid., 56-58.

18. R.M. Potter letter to H.A. McArdle, 4-5; McArdle notebook and papers, Texas State Archives.

19. Green, *El Soldado Mexicano, 1835-1836*, Military History of Texas, (undated clipping), 7; Huffines, *Blood and Noble Men*, 81-83; Sánchez Lamego, *Siege*, 33.

20. Nieto, Brown, Hefter, *El Soldado Mexicano, 1837-1847*, illustration XV.

21. Jackson, *Texas by Terán*, 14; also figure 13 and figure 14, 86.

22. Military Uniforms in America, Plate No. 321, Company of Military Historians.

## EPILOGUE

1. Roosevelt, *Memorial Edition*, vol. VIII, 131.

# *Bibliography*

**PRIMARY SOURCES**

**Archival Collections and Exhibits**

Archives and Library Division, Texas State Library. Army Correspondence and Papers. Treasury Department and Auditors Records. Quartermaster Records. McArdle notebook and letters.

Center for American History, University of Texas at Austin. Hefter (J.) Uniform sketches. Prints and Photographs Collection. Amasa Turner Papers. Moses Austin Bryan Papers. Jesse Billingsley Papers.

Chapultepec Palace Museum, Mexico, D.F., Mexico. Texas flags and artifacts.

San Jacinto Monument, La Porte, Texas. Texas uniforms and research materials.

**PUBLISHED PRIMARY MATERIALS**

**Books, Pamphlets, and Bulletins**

Blake, R.B., Comp., *Sidelights on the Battle of San Jacinto*, 2 vols. Produced by the Texas Highway Department, ca. 1939.

Bolleart, William. *William Bolleart's Texas*. Norman: University of Oklahoma Press, 1956.

Brown, Frank. *Annals of Travis County and the City of Austin*. 5 vols. Austin: typescript, Genealogy Room, Texas State Library, ca. 1875.

Coleman, Robert M. *Houston Displayed; or Who Won the Battle of San Jacinto? By a Farmer in the Army*. Velasco, 1837.

Courtney, Jovita. *After the Alamo – San Jacinto from the Notes of Dr. Nicholas Descomps Labadie*. New York, Washington, Hollywood: Vantage Press, 1964.

Delgado, Pedro. *Mexican Account of San Jacinto*. Austin: Institution for the Deaf and Dumb, 1878.

De Shields, James T. *Tall Men with Long Rifles: Set Down and Written Out by James T. De Shields as told to Him by Creed Taylor, Captain During the Texas Revolution*. San Antonio: The Naylor Co., 1935.

Dewees, William B. *Letters from an Early Settler of Texas*. Louisville: printed by the New Albany Tribune, 1858.

Ehrenberg, H(erman). *Fahren und Schicksale Eines Deutschen in Texas*, Leipsig: Verlag von Otto Wigand, 1845.In English as *With Milam and Fannin: Adventures of a German Boy in Texas' Revolution*. Translated by

Charlotte Churchill. Edited by Henry Smith. Forward by Herbert Gambrell. Dallas: Tardy Publishing Co., 1935.

Gaddy, Jerry J., comp. and ed. *Texas in Revolt: Contemporary Newspaper Account of the Texas Revolution*. Fort Collins, Colo.: Old Army Press, 1973.

Gammel, H.P.N. The Laws of Texas, 1822-1897. Austin: the Gammel Book Co., 1898.

Gray, William Fairfax. *From Virginia to Texas, 1835: Diary of Colonel William Fairfax Gray, Giving Details of His Journey to Texas and Return in 1835-1836 and Second Journey to Texas in 1837*. 1909; reprint, Houston: Fletcher Young Publishing Co., 1935 (reprint of 1845 edition).

Jackson, Jack, ed. *Texas by Terán, the Diary kept by General Manuel de Mier y Terán on his 1828 Inspection of Texas*. Translated by John Wheat. Austin: University of Texas Press, 2000.

Jenkins, John H., ed. *The Papers of the Texas Revolution, 1835-1836*. 10 vols. Austin: Presidial Press, 1973.

—. Ed. "Amasa Turner's Account of the Texas Revolution," *Texana*, vol. 1, Spring 1963, No. 2. Waco: Davis Brothers Publishing Co., 1963.

—. Ed. "Regulations of the National Militia of Coahuila and Texas, 1828." *Texas Military History and the Southwest*, vol. 7, No. 3. Austin, 1969.

Jenkins, John Holland. *Recollections of Early Texas: The Memoirs of John Holland Jenkins*. Edited by John Holmes Jenkins III. Austin: University of Texas Press, 1958.

Johnson, Frank W. *A History of Texas and Texans*. 5 vols. Edited by Eugene C. Barker. Chicago and New York: American Historical Association, 1914.

Jordan, Jonathan W. "Lone Star Republic's Navy." New York: MHQ: *The Quarterly Journal of Military History*, Autumn 1999.

Marshall, Bruce. *Uniforms of the Republic of Texas*. Atglen, Pennsylvania: Schiffer Publishing Ltd, 1999.

Maverick, George Maddison and Mary A. Maverick. *Memoirs of Mary Maverick*. San Antonio: Alamo Printing Company, 1921.

Morrell, Z.N. *Flowers and Fruits from the Wilderness or 36 Years in Texas and Seven Winters in Honduras*. Boston: Guild & Lincoln, 1872.

Peña, José Enrique de la. *With Santa Anna in Texas: a Personal Narrative of the Revolution*. Translated and edited by Carmen Perry. College Station: Texas A&M University Press, 1975.

Potter, R.M. "Escape of Karnes and Teal from Matamoros." vol. IV, Oct. 1900,

No. 2, *The Quarterly of the Texas State Historical Association*. Austin: 1900.

Santos, Richard G., ed. "Regulations for Civic Militia Coahuila and Texas, 1834." *Texas Military History*, vol. 7, No. 3. Denton, Texas, winter 1967.

Smithwick, Noah. *The Evolution of a State; or, Recollections of Old Texas Days*. Compiled by Nanna Smithwick Donaldson. 1900; reprint, Austin: University of Texas Press, 1983.

Stiff, Colonel Edward. *The Texas Emigrant, Being a Narration of the Adventures of the author in Texas, and a Description of the Soil, Climate, Productions, Minerals, Towns, Bays, Harbors, Rivers, Institutions and Manners and Customs of the Inhabitants of That Country: Together With the Principal Incidents of Fifteen Years, Revolution in Mexico: And Embracing a Condensed Statement of Interesting Events in Texas, From the First European Settlement in 1692, Down to the Year 1840.* Cincinnati. George Conclin, 1840. Waco: reprint by Texian Press, 1968.

Winfrey, Dorman and James M. Day. *The Texan Indian Papers*. 6 vols. Austin: Texas State Library, 1959-1960.

## Newspapers
*New Orleans Bee*, vol. IX, No. 50, November 21, 1835. New Orleans, 1835.

# SECONDARY MATERIALS

## Books, Pamphlets and Bulletins
Abernathy, Francis E. *Observations and Reflections on Texas Folklore*. Austin, Encino Press, 1972.

Bancroft, Hubert Howe. *History of the North Mexican States and Texas*. 2 vols. San Francisco: A.L. Bancroft and Co., 1884.

Barker, Eugene C. *The Life of Stephen F. Austin, Founder of Texas, 1793-1836. A Chapter in the Westward Movement of the Anglo-American People.* 1925; reprint, Austin: Texas State Historical Association, 1949.

—. *Mexico and Texas 1821-1835*. Dallas: P.L. Turner Co., 1928.

Bate, Walter N. *General Sidney Sherman, Texas Soldier, Statesman, and Builder*. Waco: Texian Press, 1974.

Brown, John Henry. *History of Texas from 1685 to 1892*. 2 vols. St. Louis: L.E. Daniell, 1892-1893.

Carter, Hodding. *Doomed Road of Empire*. New York: McGraw-Hill, 1963.

Chambers, William Morton. *Sketches in the Life of General Thomas Jefferson Chambers of Texas*. Galveston: Book and Job Office of *The Galveston News*, 1853.

Cisneros, Sir José, KCHS. *Riders Across the Centuries, Horseman of the Spanish Borderlands*. El Paso: Texas Western Press, 1984.

Conner, John Edwin. *Flags of Texas*. Norman: Harlow Publishing Co., 1964.

Cox, Mamie Wynne. *The Romantic Flags of Texas*. Dallas: Banks Upshaw and Co., 1936.

De Shields, James T. *They Sat in High Places: the Presidents and Governors of Texas*. San Antonio: the Naylor Co., 1940.

Dienst, Alex. *The Navy of the Republic of Texas*. Temple, Texas: 2 vols. Source Texana Series, 1909. Fort Collins, Colo.: reprint, Old Army Press, (n.d.).

*1836 The Alamo*. San Antonio: Daughters of the Republic of Texas, 1981.

Fehrenbach, T.R. *Lone Star: A History of Texas and the Texans*. New York: Macmillan Co., 1968.

Foote, Henry Stuart. *Texas and the Texans; or, Advance of the Anglo-American to the Southwest Including a History of Leading Events in Mexico, From the Conquest of Fernando Cortes to the Termination of the Texas Revolution.* 2 vols. Philadelphia: Thomas, Cowperthwait & Co., 1841.

Gambrell, Herbert Pickens. *Anson Jones: the Last President of Texas*. Austin: University of Texas Press, 1964.

Gilbert, Charles E. Jr. *A Concise History of Early Texas, as Told by its 30 Historic Flags*. Houston: Charles W. Parsons Publisher, 1964 (reprinted 1971).

Green, Michael Robert. "El Soldado Mexicano, 1835-1836." Austin: *Military History of Texas and the Southwest* (undated clipping), 5-10.

—. "Activo Batallón de Tres Villas, February-April, 1836." *Military History of Texas and the Southwest*, vol. XIV, No. 1. Austin: (undated clipping). 53-58.

Hardin, Stephen L. *Texian Iliad, a Military History of the Texas Revolution, 1835-1836*. Austin: University of Texas Press, 1994.

Haley, James L. *Texas, An Album of History*. Garden City, New York: Doubleday & Co., 1985.

Hefter, J(oseph). *The Army of the Republic of Texas*. Bellevue, Nebraska: Old Army Press, 1971.

—. *The Navy of the Republic of Texas*. Bellevue, Nebraska: Old Army Press, (n.d.).

—. *El Soldado Mexicano, 1837-1847*. Mexico, D.F., Mexico: Edíciónes Nieto. Brown. Hefter, 1958.

—, coordinator. *Cronica del Traje Militia en Mexico del Siglo XVI al XX*. No. 102, Ano XV. Mexico, D.F. Mexico. Artes de Mexico. 1968.

Hill, Jim Dan. *The Texas Navy, in Forgotten Battles and Shirtsleeve Diplomacy*. Chicago: University of Chicago Press, 1937. Austin: facsimile reproduction of the original by State House Press, 1987.

Hopewell, Clifford. *Sam Houston, Man of Destiny, a Biography*. Austin: Eakin Press, 1987.

Huffines, Alan C. *Blood of Noble Men, The Alamo, Siege & Battle, an Illustrated Chronology*. Austin: Eakin Press, 1999.

Jackson, Jack. *Los Tejanos*. Stamford, Conn.: Fantagraphics Books, Inc., 1982.

—. *Recuerdan El Alamo, the True Story of Juan N. Seguín and His Fight for Texas Independence*. Berkley: Last Gasp, 1979.

James, Marquis. *The Raven, a Biography of Sam Houston*. Indianapolis: the Bobbs-Merrill Co., 1929.

Koury, Michael J. *Arms for Texas, A Study of the Weapons of the Republic of Texas*. Fort Collins, Colo.: Old Army Press, 1973.

—. *Uniforms for Texas*. Unpublished manuscript. Fort Collins, Colo.: 1973.

Kredel, Fritz. *Soldiers of the American Army, 1775-1945*. Chicago: Henry Regenery Co., (n.d.).

Lockbaum, Jerry. "Old San Antonio, History in Pictures." *Old San Antonio, 250 Years in Pictures*. San Antonio: The Express Publishing Co., 1968.

Lindheim, Milton. *The Republic of the Rio Grande*. Waco: W.M. Morrison, bookseller, 1964.

Lord, Walter. *A Time to Stand*. New York: Harper & Brothers, 1961.

Matthews, Brigadier General Jay A., Jr. *The Ten Battle Flags of the Texas Revolution*. Austin, Presidial Press, 1975.

McDonald, Archie. *Travis*. Austin: Jenkins Publishing Company, 1976.

Morton, Ohland. *Terán and Texas, A Chapter in Texas-Mexican Relations*. Austin: Texas State Historical Association, 1948.

Myers, John Myers. *The Alamo*, Lincoln, Nebraska and London: E.P. Dutton and Co., 1948.

Nevin, David. *The Texans*. New York: Time-Life Books, 1975.

O'Connor, Kathryn Stoner. *The Presidio La Bahia del Espiritu Santo de Zuniqa, 1721 to 1846*. Austin: Von Boeckmann-Jones Co., 1969.

Proctor, Ben. *The Battle of the Alamo*. Austin: Texas State Historical Association, 1986.

Roosevelt, Theodore. *The Works of Theodore Roosevelt Memorial Edition*, 24 vols. Hermann Hagedorn, ed. New York: Charles Scribner's Sons, 1926.

Rosenfield, John, Jr. *Texas History Movies*. Illustrations by Jack Patton. Dallas: the Southwest Press, 1928.

Sánchez Lamego, Miguel A. *The Siege and Taking of the Alamo*. Some comments on the battle by J. Hefter. Translated by Consuelo Velasco. Santa Fe: Blue Feather Press for the Press of the Territorian, 1968.

Teja, Jesús de la. *A Revolution Remembered: The Memoirs and Selected Correspondence of Juan N. Seguín*. Austin: State House Press, 1991.

*Texas Citizen Soldiers*, Washington, Tex.: flyer by the Star of the Republic Museum, (n.d.).

Steffen, Randy. *The Horse Soldier 1776-1943*. 3 vols. Norman: University of Oklahoma Press, 1978.

*Under Texas Skies*. Vol. 1, No. 10, Austin: Texas State Historical Association, March 1951.

Tinkle, Lon. *Thirteen Days to Glory*. College Station, Texas: Texas A&M University, 1958.

Tolbert, Frank X. *The Day of San Jacinto*. New York: McGraw-Hill Book Co., 1959.

Webb, Walter Prescott, ed., *The Handbook of Texas*. 2 vols. Austin: Texas State Historical Association, 1952.

Weems, John Edward and Jane Weems. *Dreams of Empire, A Human History of the Republic of Texas 1836-1846*. New York: Simon & Schuster, 1971.

Wells, Thomas Henderson. *Commodore Moore and the Texas Navy*. Austin: University of Texas Press, 1960.

Wharton, Clarence. *Remember Goliad*. Glorietta, N.M.: Rio Grande Press, 1931 and 1968.

—. *The Republic of Texas, from the First American Colonies in 1821 to Annexation in 1846*. Houston: C.C. Young Printing Company, 1922.

Wilcox, R. Turner. *The Mode in Hats and Headdress*. New York: Charles Scribner's Sons, 1948.

Winfrey, Dorman et al. *Six Flags of Texas*. Waco: Texian Press, 1968.

Wortham, Louis J. *A History of Texas from Wilderness to Commonwealth*. 5 vols. Fort Worth: Wortham-Molyneaux Co., 1924.

Yoakum, Henderson. *History of Texas From Its First Settlement in 1685 to Its Annexation to the United States in 1846*. 2 vols. New York: J.S. Redfield, 1855.

**Articles**

Howren, Alleine. "Causes and origin of the Decree of April 6, 1830." *Southwestern Historical Quarterly.*, Vol. LXXXIII, No. 4, April 1980, 378-422.

Jenkins, William H. "The Red Rovers of Alabama." *The Alabama Review*, 106-110, April 1965.

Scarborough, Jewel Davis. "The Georgia Battalion in the Texas Revolution, a Critical Study." *The Southwestern Historical Quarterly*, Vol. LXIII, 511-532, 1960.

**Newspapers**

"Mexican officials lose Alamo flag." *Austin American Statesman*, December 19, 1994.

"Poll shows Texans allegiance to state," *Austin American Statesman*, July 24, 1997.

*Galveston News*, June 23, 1855.

**THESES AND DISERTATIONS**

Adams, Allen E. "The Leaders of the Volunteer Grays: the life of William G. Cooke, 1808-1847." M.A. thesis, Southwest Texas Teachers College, 1939.

Friend, Lorena B. "The Life of Thomas Jefferson Chambers." M.A. thesis, University of Texas at Austin, 1928.

**UNIFORM PLATES**

Hefter, J(oseph). *Uniforms of the Militia of Coahuila y Texas*, Military History Institute, Mexico, D.F., Mexico, (n.d.).

—. Elting, John R. Plate No. 321, Military Uniforms in America. The Company of Military Historians. Westport, Conn.: 1973.

Jones, Tom. *Alabama Red Rovers, 1835*. Plate No. 502, Military Uniforms in America. The Company of Military Historians, Westport, Conn.: 1980.

—. *The First Texas Rangers, 1823*. Plate No. 457, Military Uniforms in America. The Company of Military Historians. Westport, Conn.: 1977.

—. Elting, John R. *The Alamo Garrison, March 1836*. Plate No. 386, Military Uniforms in America. The Company of Military Historians. Westport, Conn.: 1973.

**INTERVIEWS AND PERSONAL COMMUNICATIONS**

Biffle, Kent. Texana columnist, *The Dallas Morning News*. Interview by author, November 14, 1994.

Elting, Colonel John R., USA (Ret.) Texana expert, Company of Military Historians, to author, March 25, 1995. Letter in author's possession.

Green, Michael. Austin, Texas. Former Reference Archivist, Texas State Archives, former Assistant Editor, *Military History of Texas and the Southwest*. Telephone interviews by author September 24, 1994, January 5, 1995, February 2, 1995. Letter of May 20, 1994 to Bruce Marshall, in author's possession.

Hefter, Joseph. Mexico, D.F., Mexico and Cuernavaca, Mexico. Artist and military historian. Interview by author in Mexico City September 17, 1972. Letter to author December 13, 1972 in author's possession.

Koury, Michael J. Fort Collins, Colo. Editor and publisher, Old Army Press. Telephone interview by author, February 3, 1998.

Matthews, Brigadier General Jay A., Jr. editor and publisher, Presidial Press, editor emeritus, *Military History of the West* (formerly *Military History of Texas and the Southwest*). Numerous telephone interviews by author, 1994, 1995, 1996.

Miller, Edward. San Antonio. High school history teacher with special interest and research concerning the New Orleans Grays to author May 19, 1995. Letter and enclosures in author's possession.

Milligan, Edward. Alexandria, VA. Texana specialist, Company of Military Historians to author June 17, 1994. Letters in author's possession.

Nesmith, Sam. San Antonio. Former curator of the Alamo and former researcher for the University of Texas Institute of Texan Cultures at San Antonio. Telephone interview by author August 25, 1995.

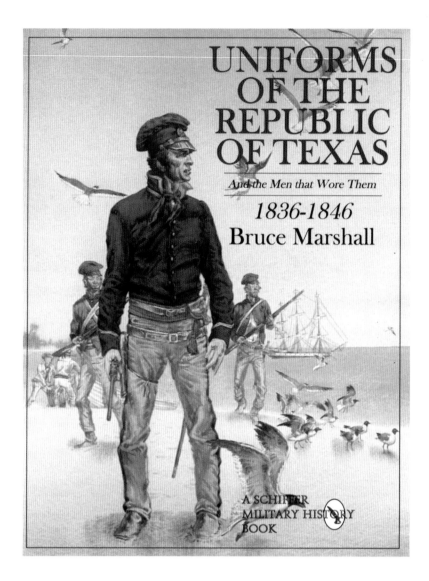

# Uniforms of the Republic of Texas
## And the Men that Wore Them 1836-1846

### Bruce Marshall

Only Texas, of all the states, can boast of a heritage that includes the army and navy of an independent nation. Its regulars were backed up by a militia described as "the most formidable, for their numbers, in the world." Contrary to the image projected by Hollywood and most historians, even in Texas, they were smartly uniformed and equipped with the latest in weaponry. With his internationally-honored art, Bruce Marshall has recreated the uniforms in full color illustrations, supplemented by fourteen photographs – including the only two known of uniformed officers of the Texas army and navy.

Size: 8 1/2" x 11" • 26 color plates, over 30 b/w images • 88 pp.
ISBN: 0-7643-0682-0 • soft cover • $19.95